Neck Tales

Neck Tales

Stories from Virginia's Northern Neck

By Thea Marshall

Brandylane Publishers, Inc.

ISBN: 978-1-883911-86-7
Library of Congress Control Number: 2009928130

The following essays were previously published in *Pleasant Living* magazine (www.pleasantlivingmagazine.com)
Strat-by-the-Ford. May/June 2008
Tomatoes. March/April 2008

A version of the following essays were previously published in *Baysplash Magazine* (www.baysplash.com)
Barleycorn. Volume V, Issue 2
Blue Highways. Volume V, Issue 1
Community Newspapers. Volume IV, Issue 3
Of Kings and Citizens. Volume IV, Issue 4
A Look Into Fithian's Journal. Volume VI, Issue 3
The Most Notable Mother of Us All. Volume VI, Issue 2
Our Boy Harry. Volume V, Issue 3
Poets, Presidents and Patriots. Volume VI, Issue 1
The Queens of the Northern Neck. Volume IV, Issue 4
Yeocomico Church, Through the Wicket Door. Volume VI, Issue 2

Brandylane Publishers, Inc.
Richmond, Virginia
www.brandylanepublishers.com

Printed in the United States of America

To my mother ... Her voice now still, her sweet spirit alive
in everything that is good in this world

Contents

In the Beginning. The Crossroads.

The town of Kilmarnock, the refreshed business hub of today's Northern Neck of Virginia, and occupying less than three square miles, has enough history, and some say intrigue, surrounding its early days, to keep genealogists and historians busy for quite a while. For my part, as neither a historian nor genealogist but merely a Northern Necker with an intense interest in beginnings, the town's early years conjure up endless musings.

Back in the 1600s, it was simply "the crossroads," named for a pair of Indian paths crisscrossing each other. Then, with a population growing with all manner of folks, from hardy pioneers to indentured servants, there came to be farms, storehouses, and those earliest of what we might think of as "bed and breakfast" rest stops and tavern called "ordinaries." The very first ordinary was Steptoe's, named after its proprietor, William Steptoe. Inevitably, the little town became "Steptoe's," but I'm getting ahead of myself.

William Steptoe was the grandson of Anthony Steptoe, who came to the Neck in the 1600s with that early band of adventurers as an indentured servant. He worked his way out of his six-year debt and lived to grandfather that very first Northern Neck entrepreneur, William. Recently, the business owners on Main Street, believing, I guess, that everything old is new, have decided to call the downtown business district

Steptoe's in honor of that very first known business owner, William Steptoe, grandson of Anthony.

But we still haven't arrived at the present name, Kilmarnock. Stories abound as to how that name came about. One that has gained the most credence points to a Mr. Robert Gilmour. I learned about Gilmour from Brainard Edmonds' little book about Kilmarnock, *A Virginia Town and Its People*. Mr. Gilmour came to the area in the mid 1700s as an agent for a Scottish mercantile firm. He is said to have owned property in Kilmarnock, Scotland, and perhaps it made him feel more at home to call the little corner of his new world in Virginia, Kilmarnock.

Today, the Virginia and Scottish towns of Kilmarnock consider themselves sister cities. The Virginia Kilmarnock even has its Scottish Days celebrations, though I personally think the Northern Neck should have an additional celebration: an annual Anthony Steptoe Day, to celebrate the man who arrived here in the Neck centuries ago as an indentured servant and set the pattern for what I like to think of as the possibilities of re-invention. Whether a born-here, a been-here, a come-here, or come-back-here, history tells us that "here" is the land where you can be just about anything you strive to be; "here," the land of pioneers and presidents; "here," the land which for centuries has been called "the land of pleasant living." "Here" is also the land of re-inventors.

Historic Christ Church and Its Early Parishioners, and a Woman of Mystery

I live just about two miles from the beautifully restored historic Christ Church here in the Northern Neck, and, of course, pass it many, many times, always noting the simple grandeur of the structure. Built by Robert "King" Carter and completed in 1735, it seems to hold down a special corner of the Northern Neck. It's always an adventure to explore the church and grounds and spectacular herb gardens; all is kept in good order by members of the Historic Christ Church Foundation. It's a living church, still used today for weddings and funeral and memorial services.

I've often wondered about those early parishioners, some of whom probably lived on the land I call mine. What were their lives like, and did they all come to this church and pray together? Many answers can be found in a terrific set of books researched by volunteers of the foundation. One volume tells us that some folks were the landed gentry and wealthy plantation owners, and, of course, that included the Carter clan. They were at the tip of the pyramid; in the middle were the small landholders, the largest group; the base of the pyramid was made up of white and black craftsmen, black slaves, white indentured servants, landless white laborers, some free blacks and some Native Americans.

Another volume, *People in Profile*, does just that, profiling fourteen families who lived in the parish between 1720 and 1750. You won't be surprised that my favorite profile is that of "Rebecca Banton, Mysterious Woman of Wealth." It was difficult for the researchers to learn about women of that era because, well, following English law, we simply weren't people then. Women lived under the rule of their fathers, husbands, guardians or other males. But there was an uncommon amount of information about Rebecca.

I'll cut to the quick: she had a bad-man dad. He was summoned to court a number of times for ungentlemanly behavior, but she inherited his worldly goods, which were a lot, and some say ill gotten. She disappears from the records for three decades; then there comes to light this stunning fact: Miss Rebecca becomes the principal heir of a well-to-do bachelor, Henry Fleet III, from one of the county's most prominent families, and when he died, she came into the use of his estate, making her "the most comfortably situated woman in Christ Church parish."

You can learn lots more about Miss Rebecca in this sweet set of books, and all about that bachelor and his family's descendants currently living, it is believed, right here in Lancaster county. The books are available at the gift shop at Historic Christ Church in Irvington. It's worth the trip.

Of Kings and Citizens

Once upon a time, here on the Northern Neck of Virginia, we had a King. Well, a so-called King: Robert "King" Carter, born 1663, died 1732. I live on land originally owned by his father and then by him; but to be accurate, just about everyone who lives here on the Neck lives on land once owned by Robert "King" Carter, since he owned thousands and thousands of acres.

You probably know something about him. He was the richest man, owned the most slaves, grew the most tobacco, and like many Kings, real or so-called, he had lots of descendants—as many as 65,000, for goodness sake! He is renowned for the creation of the now historic and exquisitely restored Christ Church sitting between Irvington and Weems.

My favorite of "King" Carter's 65,000 descendants (though I don't know more than a handful) is Robert Carter the Third of Nomini. I don't know much about the other 64,999, but Bobby the Third should be better known than he is. Besides inheriting tremendous wealth, making him a land-rich planter, he became a banker, ship owner, and merchant. His home, Nomini Hall, was on more than 1,000 acres in Westmoreland County. Today, many of those acres serve as a rich archaeological dig for university students.

Carter owned a huge library for the time and an eclectic collection of musical instruments, some of them coveted by

Thomas Jefferson. He was a buddy of King George III, but became a true American patriot during the Revolution and even had his slaves make socks for George Washington's army. Later on, he had what today might be called a mid-life crisis combined with some extraordinary spiritual experiences. He had left the Church of England earlier in his life, but now he embraced Arminianism. Since one of their beliefs is that we are all equal under God, it should not have been as stunning as it was that for reasons both ethical and perhaps economic, Carter devised a simple plan to free his more than five hundred slaves over a period of time beginning in 1791.

All who knew him, or thought they knew him, were scandalized, which affected him not at all, for along with this move he happily exchanged his earned titles, which included colonel, vestryman, and others, for one he proudly gave himself: "Citizen"—just like the other 64,999 of his relatives and all the rest of us here on the Northern Neck.

Blue Highways

I've been re-reading a book called *Blue Highways*. It was written in the early 80s by William Least Heat-Moon. That's his Osage name; his Irish-English name is William Trogdon. Dr. William Trogdon, a professor of English at a university in Missouri. His book at the time was a kind of a cult book for road adventurers. The title comes from the old highway maps, where the main routes were printed in red and the back ones in blue.

After losing his job at the university, he decided to drive around the country on the blue highways, stopping where the name of a town seemed interesting or intriguing. He started from Missouri and made a circle of 13,000 miles that took him through towns ranging from Bad Ax and Ball Club to White Salmon and Why. He stopped to chat with folks, learn the history and sometimes the mystery of the towns, and sample the food when he could find what he called a "three calendar café." This referred to what he called his "almost infallible way to find honest food at just prices in Blue Highway America: count the wall calendars in a café. According to his informal research,

No calendar: Same as an Interstate pit stop.
One calendar: Pre-processed food assembled in New Jersey.

Two calendars: Only if fish trophies present.
Three calendars: Can't miss on the farm-boy
breakfasts.
Four calendars: Try the ho-made pie too.
Five calendars: Keep it under your hat, or they'll
franchise.

For good reason, food played a major role in his journey.
It broke the monotony and gave him the chance to talk to
strangers and learn about the towns he found himself in.

Naturally I thought of the blue highways of the Northern
Neck, but of course, all the highways, or rather, roads, of the
Northern Neck are blue, and they run through towns with
interesting names like Alfonso and Dogue. Years ago, driving
through the town of Lively was always a cause for hilarity when
my youngsters spotted the sign announcing "Grumpy's Pizza."

The roads of the Neck have a long history, as does the Neck
itself. At first, there was really no need for roads, or paths as
they were called, because everyone lived on the water, and travel
was by boat; but soon there were inland tobacco plantations
and the planters needed roads to get to the wharves. Narrow
paths were built, just wide enough for hogsheads of tobacco
fitted with axles to be rolled, pushed or pulled to the wharves
so that they could get, ultimately, to their destinations overseas.
In 1658 the General Assembly mandated that the roads must
be forty feet wide and that the citizens were to be responsible
for their upkeep. In Miriam Haynie's wonderful book about the
Northern Neck, *The Stronghold*, she writes, "This order was hard
to enforce because for a long time the planters had little interest
in highways on land."

Sometimes it's hard to realize how much has changed since
1658. Today we have countless land highways. Those red and
blue lines on the map seem like threads, sewing this nation

together.

The closest Least Heat-Moon got to the Neck on that early trip was Smith Island, Maryland. If he had come a bit closer he would have discovered good eateries, with and without calendars, and interesting folk anxious and willing to talk about their unique towns, but he would have made another discovery: that we on the Neck have two sets of blue highways: the winding land roads which have been here for centuries, and the other ones, the ageless blue highways, the rivers and creeks that are so much of what make the Northern Neck, well, the Northern Neck. I suspect it would have added even more meaning to his response when asked what he learned from his odyssey. "I did learn what I didn't know I wanted to know."

An Eighteenth Century Man and a Twenty-First Century Connection

The name Community Idea Stations, used by the Richmond-based National Public Radio station and its sister stations, has always delighted me. I think their best idea to date, the one that most exemplifies the "community idea station" notion, is the tower in Heathsville, here in the Northern Neck, enabling this area to receive their radio programming. Now, why they chose Heathsville, I'm not sure—perhaps because of its central location—but I like to think it has to do with John Heath, for whom, of course, the town is named.

When John Heath was born in 1758, it was just Wicomico Parish in Northumberland County. Just as the station is an idea station, John Heath was an idea man. When he was a student at William and Mary, he got a terrific idea: he and a few friends would start a club. Now most of us in our lifetime have known someone who's said, "Hey, let's start a club," and it got started and fizzled out after a year or so. Not so with John Heath and friends. Their club, or rather, society, was founded on December 5, 1776 and it had it all: an oath of secrecy, badge, mottos, initiations, special handclasp, and regular meetings, where the main topics were literary, particularly composition and debating. John Heath of Heathsville became its first president, and under him one of the first debates was "Whether a wise State hath any Interest nearer at Heart than the Education of the Youth." The name of the society was Phi Beta Kappa.

John Heath and most of the other early members (there were fifty at the beginning) later distinguished themselves as great public servants. Heath served in the Revolutionary War, was admitted to the bar, practiced law in Northumberland County, served as Commonwealth Attorney, served in the House of Delegates, was elected to the Third Congress, was appointed a member of the Virginia Privy Council in 1803 and moved to Richmond, where he died seven years later.

What hasn't died is Phi Beta Kappa. Today there are chapters at 270 colleges and universities with over half a million invited members. *Phi*, *beta*, and *kappa* are the Greek initials of the motto "love of learning is the guide of life." I think John Heath, whom I call the Idea Man, would have been more than a little pleased to discover the Community Idea Stations, with their love of learning, making themselves at home on his turf.

Rappahannock Tribe Road Marker

There are about 1,500 historic site road markers in Virginia, those steel gray signs popping up periodically, like square gray flowers, near a site that the state has declared, well, historic. Many are in the Northern Neck, commemorating everything from the birth of now-famous men and women, to special places and events that are central to the history of the Neck. Some are on seemingly unlikely, even inappropriate, sites. One of my favorite "unlikelies" is on a street corner in Kilmarnock, a few feet from an old gas station. It reads, in part, "Here was born Oct. 25, 1817, Henrietta Hall, first American woman missionary to China."

One of the Northern Neck's newest markers is most appropriate and overdue. It recognizes the presence of the Rappahannock Indians in Richmond County. There was a kind of "unveiling" event that took place at the Ruritan park on Totuskey Creek. The marker reads,

> Prior to the 17th century, the Rappahannock Indians maintained seasonal residences on the banks of Totuskey Creek. They fished for spawning shad and herring each spring, trapping fish in the creek's narrows and preparing them for the tribe to consume or trade. When the Rappahannocks were forced to begin selling their lands to the English in 1651,

12

part of the tribe moved here to "Totosha" Town. In 1667, the Rappahannocks sold this town and moved to their hunting grounds on the south side of the Rappahannock River where they continue to live today.

Totuskey Creek is in Richmond County, one of the counties of the Northern Neck.

Francine Barber is the director of the Richmond County Museum. She and her husband, John Barber Sr., and, of course, the museum itself are major resources for history buffs. The Barbers told me a bit more about the Rappahannock Indians. When Capt. John Smith explored and mapped the Rappahannock River region in 1608, he found that what is now Richmond County was occupied by the great Rappahannock Indians, members of the Powhatan Confederacy.

The Rappahannocks were a powerful tribe with fourteen villages around the river, one of which was near the mouth of Totuskey Creek. As colonial settlements increased, the Rappahannocks moved to the upper reaches of the creeks. A 1677 treaty established a 3,474-acre Rappahannock reservation on the south side of the river. Although that area lost reservation status a few years later, the Rappahannocks continued to occupy the area.

And their descendants have founded the Rappahannock Tribe Cultural Center at Indian Neck in King and Queen County. It's worth the trip, and so is the Richmond County Museum. The museum is located in the old jail (c. 1872) on the courthouse green. The courthouse itself is the oldest continuously operating courthouse in America; and it's right here in the Northern Neck.

Our Boy Harry

Hundreds of years before an English boy named Harry was born in the wondrous and fertile imagination of J.K. Rowling, the Northern Neck was visited by a very real English boy named Harry. History tells us his name was actually Henry Spelman, but he was more often than not called Harry, and that he was the third son of Sir Henry Spelman, a scholar, historian and expert on medieval manuscripts.

Harry left home at the age of fourteen to board a ship to Jamestown, and arrived there in 1609. Did the lad run away from home? If so, why? Could it be because, as a third son, primogeniture reared its frequently unfair head, and therefore gave him little in the way of inheritance to look forward to? Or did his father send him to this new world as a punishment—or as a reward?

This too seems to be a mystery, though perhaps a clue can be found in the opening sentence of an incredible document written by Henry Spelman, while still a lad: "Beinge in displeasuer of my frendes, and desirous to see other cuntryes, after [sum weekes], three moneths sayle we cum with prosperus winds in sight of Virginia."

"Being in displeasure of my friends!" What indeed could that have meant? It boggles the mind to contemplate what misadventures could have caused him to leave his hometown in England at fourteen, board a ship that would cross an ocean, headed for what?

But once here, his adventures, misadventures, experiences and exploits come close to rivaling that other English, albeit fictional, boy, Harry Potter. For me, there are other delicious parallels to the Harry Potter stories, whose main characters include a trio of teenagers. If you are a fan, you know that Harry P. has two sidekicks, Ron and Hermione. Well, there was another real life lad who was about our real life Harry's age, who arrived in Jamestown a bit earlier than Harry Spelman, listed on the passenger list as Thomas Savage, "boy laborer," and their paths crossed a number of times. If you are as much a besotted Potter fan as I, it takes a very short stretch to cast Savage, at least for a while, in the role of Ron. And who plays the part of Hermione in this very real drama? Hold on to your feathers!!! Of course, it's Pocahontas.

Real life adventures? How's this for starters? Not long after arriving in Jamestown, Spelman is taken along on an expedition by Capt. John Smith to meet the great Indian chief, Powhatan, and then, according to one account, Smith traded the lad to the Indian chief for a town! Or, as another account reports, he was left there by Smith to learn the ways and languages of the Indians. Now for the boy's own words: "I was caried By Capt Smith our Presidant to ye Fales, to ye litell Powhatan wher unknowne to me he sould me to him for a towne caled Powhatan and leavinge me with him ye litle Powhatann, He made knowne to Capt weste how he had bought a toune for them to dwell in...." In more modern words, "I was carried by Capt. Smith our president to the little Powhatan where unknown to me he sold me to him for a town called Powhatan..., and leaving me with him he made known to Capt. West how he had bought a town for them to dwell in."

According to early writings, not long after his arrival, there was a village massacre, and Harry was saved by none other than Hermione—sorry, I mean Princess Pocahontas—and it is believed by many that they escaped to, where else, the Northern Neck and the land of "King Po-tow-meek." Though he was more a prisoner than guest, he lived with the Indians there and learned much about them and, most importantly, became a first-rate interpreter of their languages.

Two years later, when an English ship arrived captained by Samuel Argall, Argall traded a large supply of copper to the Indians in exchange for Harry. Here are more of Harry's own words:

> Capt. Argall...understoo*d* that ther was an english boy named Harry. He desiringe to here further of me cam up the river w*hi*ch the Kinge of Patomeck hearringe sent me to him an*d* I goinge backe agayne brought the kinge to him ye shipe, wher capt: Argall gave the Kinge sum copper for me, w*hi*ch he receyved Thus was I sett free at libertye and brought into England.

In those two years with the Indians our Harry became wise, it would seem, beyond his years. Back in England Spelman wrote "The Relation of Virginia," an amazing work from a relatively unschooled boy. All the quotes I have used are from that document, which is thought to be the first recorded description of the Northern Neck. Here are more of those words:

> The country is full of wood in some parts, and water they have plentiful. They have marsh ground, and small fields for corn, and other grounds whereon their deer, goats, and stags..., with fish in abundance whereon they live most part of the summertime.

How remarkable that so much remains unchanged on our Northern Neck four hundred years later!

In 1616, Henry Spelman, our boy Harry, came back to Virginia and was, quite sensibly, given the job of Indian interpreter. There are more adventures to come that include a possible betrayal by his sometimes buddy, Thomas Savage, who was also an interpreter for the colonists. (And if that act of betrayal were true, would that end any resemblance of Potter's friend, Ron, to Savage?) The end to Harry Spelman's story is in itself like a work of fiction. Unlike some reviewers of the last of the Harry Potter series, I will try not be a "spoiler." Therefore I leave his story here, for you to enjoy the adventure of research and discover for yourself how the life of our very own English boy named Harry, Henry Spelman, came to an end.

The Most Notable Mother of Us All

She has been called the most sacred and noble character among women in the annals of American history. Here in the Northern Neck, her strength, independence, and presence still reign. A cousin of hers said, "I could not behold that remarkable woman without feelings, it is impossible to describe."

Who was that "remarkable woman," a woman of such dynamic presence that Lafayette is said to have likened her to a Roman matron? Mary Ball Washington, the mother of the man called the father of his country. She was born in Lancaster County in 1708 and orphaned by the time she was thirteen. She was widowed at thirty-five, with five children, left to be our nation's most famous single mother. That she had a profound influence on her first born is absolutely undisputed, though there are those amateur psychologists who bicker about the mother-son relationship, and whether George was an attentive and loving son or not. Reading some of his letters home seems to stoke the fires of ire. This is an excerpt from one of the letters Washington wrote to his mother after she expressed a need for funds after going on about his huge expenses. He writes,

> I do not, however, offer it as any excuse for not paying you what may really be due; for let this be little or much, I am willing, however unable, to pay to the

utmost farthing; but it is really hard upon me when you have taken every thing you wanted from the plantation by which money could be raised, when I have not received one farthing, directly nor indirectly from the place for more than twelve years, if ever....

Other letters show a real effort to keep his mother informed about his battles. The following is from a long letter written in 1755 after a terrible battle:

The Virginia troops shew'd a good deal of bravery, and were near all kill'd; the dastardly behaviour of those they call regular's expos'd all others that were inclin'd to do their duty to almost certain death; and at last they broke and run as sheep pursued by dogs; and it was impossible to rally them. I luckily escap'd with't [without] a wound, tho' I had four bullets through my coat, and two horses shot under me.

Gosh, how reassuring for Mom! On the other hand, he did express much concern about her living alone, and often tried to persuade her to live with daughter Betty. She refused, and lived independently until her death. In one of her letters she expressed this independence quite poignantly. She wrote, "If I ever be driven this way again, I will go into some little house of my own, if it is only twelve feet square." Here's to you, dear Mrs. Washington.

Our Founders' Faiths

I have had the privilege and pleasure of meeting and interviewing author, biographer and historian, Prof. Alf J. Mapp Jr. on three or four occasions. His books on Thomas Jefferson are considered national treasures, and we in the Northern Neck consider him one of our treasures (he lived here part time for many, many years). One of his most interesting books is *The Faiths of Our Fathers: What America's Founders Really Believed*. A definition of that word "faith" may be a good starting point.

Faith: belief in god or the doctrines or teaching of religion; a system of religious belief.

Prof. Mapp points out that it was believed that a number of the Founding Fathers were deists and embraced no particular religion. Two of the Founding Fathers Prof. Mapp writes about that have roots in the Northern Neck are George Washington and James Madison.

About Washington, Prof. Mapp wrote that some mystery surrounds George Washington's attitude toward religion. Was Washington a deist, or what? Professor Mapp cites many reported instances of Washington's thanking providence for his victories, and much evidence of religious conviction in the way in which Washington met the challenges of his life. Much of the mystery seems to stem from the fact that Washington refrained from taking communion. Prof. Mapp suggests that perhaps this great man felt unworthy of taking communion?

Going on to James Madison, the Father of the Constitution, author with Alexander Hamilton of *The Federalist*: this tiny dynamo was certain he would die in his twenties, but lived into his eighties. Was he a deist? As a student at Princeton, he advocated the separation of church and state, and throughout his life he was a zealous guardian of religious freedom. Prof. Mapp tells us that this is a frequently overlooked aspect of his presidency. Prof. Mapp has written that there are no detailed records of Madison's belief, but that there are certain things we do know. He was no atheist; he was certainly Christian, and held fast to the idea that nothing in life was more important than religion and that religion could never become irrelevant. James Madison was one of many of our Founding Fathers who were free of any bigoted assumption that those of other religions were automatically inferior. His reason told him that the truth was otherwise. The tradition of tolerance remains alive and well in today's Northern Neck.

James Madison's Slaves

If you own a home in the Northern Neck, it's possible that your property, or at least, the land, was once land belonging to slaveholders. It is possible that folks living not too far from your home are descendants of the slaves who worked the land so long ago. Though I have lived here a very long time, I still find this startling. Then, when I learned that descendants of African Americans who had been enslaved at President James Madison's plantation, Montpelier, held an annual reunion, and that the mission of the reunion was to "commemorate and honor the contributions of those whose freedom was sacrificed to build our nation," I wanted to learn more about one of the Northern Neck's born-here presidents and his views on slavery. And I did—but it raised far more questions than it answered.

Here's what Madison had to say in a speech at the Constitutional Convention, June 1787: "We have seen the mere distinction of color made in the most enlightened period of time, a ground of the most oppressive dominion ever exercised by man over man." Yet we learn that there were more than 100 slaves at Montpelier at the time of Madison's death. To explain this ambivalence, this contradiction in thought and deed, Pulitzer Prize-winning author, historian and civil rights leader Roger Wilkins was a speaker at one of the reunions. Shortly afterwards, in an interview with National Public Radio, Prof. Wilkins said he learned that he was a descendant of Madison's slaves from his grandmother, who, he said, grew up on the Northern Neck.

The interview sent me back to Wilkins' book, *Jefferson's Pillow*. In the book, he looks at the paradox of the written and spoken words of our Founding Fathers versus their actions by exploring the lives of George Washington, George Mason, James Madison, and Thomas Jefferson. He says in his book, "Their class, education, and personality somehow permitted them to live with the institution of slavery." He continues by describing how he felt while standing at the foot of the Jefferson Memorial in Washington: "I am puzzled as I stare up at the image of this man who wrote that his earliest memory was of being carried on a pillow by a slave riding on horseback, and who at the time of his death still owned well over a hundred human beings upon whom, somehow, he had been unwilling or unable to bestow the blessings of liberty.

I don't know if the people at the Montpelier reunion, the descendants of slaves, passed judgment on Madison and the other Founding Fathers, but here is what Roger Wilkins wrote: "We are obliged to judge; to probe the flaws of our predecessors is to engage not in vindictive finger-pointing but to resist hubris and complacency in our own time."

Words to ponder in our own time.

The Underrated President

Here's an anomaly for you. A man considered to have been, say the historians, the most qualified in his time to become president, has been the most underrated. Who was this Northern Neck native son? Well, here's a clue: other than George Washington, he was the only early patriot who would become president to have fought in the Revolutionary War, and he was the last of our earliest presidents to have been born in Virginia.

He was James Monroe, born in Westmoreland County in the Northern Neck, where folks celebrated his 250th birthday in 2008. A quick search of the Internet gives us an idea of some of the notable events of his term, some more notable than others.

Congress decided on thirteen as the number of stripes on the flag representing the original colonies; the boundary between Canada and the United States was fixed at the 49th parallel; Spain ceded Florida to the United States in exchange for the cancellation of $5 million in Spanish debt; the Missouri Compromise admitted Missouri as a slave state, but forbade slavery in any states carved from the Louisiana Territory north of thirty-six degrees thirty minutes latitude.

By the end of his first term, scholars tell us, Monroe's administration was known for its idealism and integrity. His personal popularity was at an all-time high—so high that running for his second term was a cakewalk. He carried every state and received every electoral vote except one, cast by a New Hampshire elector for John Quincy Adams, who, by the way, was Monroe's secretary of state.

In spite of his enormous popularity, he had an especially virulent enemy, Aaron Burr. According to historians, Monroe was merely one of many on Burr's enemies list. Why? Well, apparently Burr had come to a time in his life when he seemed to have hated and distrusted just about everyone.

President James Monroe is probably most remembered for what is known as the Monroe Doctrine, the doctrine that proclaimed that foreign powers were no longer to colonize or interfere with the affairs of our newly independent nation. While it's named for him, many others in his cabinet contributed to it, especially his secretary of state, John Quincy Adams.

The subject of slavery and our early presidents' attitude towards slavery has to be addressed. Harry Ammon, who is a noted Monroe historian, has said that Monroe (and the others) had two views on slavery that were at odds with each other: a public view for the reduction of slavery, and a private world that depended on it. Monroe was a supporter of colonization for freed American slaves and was honored for this when the capital of Liberia, Monrovia, was named for him. It is probable that Monroe was as tormented by the slavery issue as were the presidents who preceded him, because he was, first and foremost, a decent man. Thomas Jefferson said of him, "Monroe was so honest that if you turned his soul inside out there would not be a spot on it."

President James Monroe, born more than two and a half centuries ago, right here, on the Northern Neck.

Closing the Gap

A museum's primary purpose is to safeguard and preserve our heritage and culture. Here in the Northern Neck there are sixteen museums working to do just that. One of them, the Mary Ball Washington Museum in Lancaster County, has completed phase one of a unique project that has gained some national attention. The project's official title: "Black Virginians in the Northern Neck: Closing a Gap in American History."

From amateur history buffs to professional genealogists to, maybe, you and me, people have been on a quest, trying to trace their roots. Who might they find in their family tree? Down here, it could be anyone from a plantation owner to a president, indentured servant or slave. For most of us, of course, we find just plain folks. Even so, they're our plain folks and the history and mystery of our past intrigues us. But there has been a gap, a wide gap, filled with the many untold stories and the rich history of African Americans, slaves, soldiers, seamen, and free men—and women.

The museum has completed the oral history phase, so that today you can go to the museum and listen to the recorded conversations of some fifty men and women whose memories include the stories and conversations of the tragedies and triumphs of long-ago family members and events. There is simply nothing like listening to history from the perspectives of the people who lived it, or who can recall talking with friends and family who did.

The second phase of the project is a genealogical study of at least ten local African-American families whose ancestors fought on land or sea as patriots in the American Revolution. I recently read about a slave named Caesar who piloted *The Patriot*, a Virginia ship on which other black seamen had served. Imagine finding evidence that a real hero was a part of your family history. Perhaps that's one of the reasons so many of us go "a'searching," in the hopes of finding a hero or heroine in our past. Wouldn't that make the present seem filled with new possibilities from the past?

Poets, Presidents and Patriots

The Northern Neck is well known for being the birthplace of presidents and patriots. Less known is that the area has been home to poets, playwrights, and even poet presidents. A sample of the creative efforts of our best-known born-here president, President Washington, found in one of his earliest notebooks, goes like this:

> Ah! woe's me that I should Love and conceal,
> Long have I wish'd, but never dare reveal,
> Even though severely Love's Pains I feel;
> Xerxes that great, wasn't free from Cupids Dart,
> And all the greatest Heroes, felt the smart.

Many believe that George Washington wrote that when he was a love-struck teenager; others believe that he copied it from an obscure book of poems into his notebook. This is only one of the two known poems he may have written, and there's no record of any later forays into poetry. President James Madison, another of the Neck's born-here presidents, wrote a few poems, one against the Tories.

> Come noble Whigs, disdain these sons
> Of screech owls, monkeys, & baboons
> Keep up you[r] minds to humourous themes

And verdant meads & flowing streams
Until this tribe of dunces find
The baseness of their groveling mind

It's said that President Madison didn't think much of his own poetry, and we're grateful that he turned his talents to politics and prose. He is, after all, the Father of our Constitution.

Today, there are scores of living, writing poets on the Northern Neck. Some have had their work published in Virginia magazines like *Pleasant Living* and *BaySplash*; some have published collections of their work. Of course, there are far more that go unpublished, but are enjoyed in a variety of ways; poetry readings abound here.

My interest in Northern Neck poets was sparked by a phone call from a woman who lived most of her eighty years in Kilmarnock, and now lives in Fork Union, Virginia. She had been searching for a poem that she had been required to memorize as a youngster, in elocution class. She clearly remembered the last line of each of the stanzas: "…in the good old Northern Neck." And that was enough to send me to the web. I "Googled" that line, and Eureka! Up it came!

Between the yellow Rappahannock
And by the broad Potomac blue
There's a lovely bit of country
Down in old Virginia true.
Just a narrow strip of inland
On the map it's scarce a speck
But it's home to everybody,
In the good old Northern Neck.

It goes on for five more stanzas, and was written about 1925 by James S. Allen. Who was Mr. Allen? Where did he come from? Where did he go? It's been easier to find obscure poems by our presidents than to find any trace of Mr. Allen, but I'm searching, "in the good old Northern Neck."

Band of Brothers

The phrase "band of brothers" has been used to depict singers, athletes, war heroes and more, but for me, the most exciting band of brothers were five men who helped shape this country from its earliest days: the Lee Boys, born at Stratford, in Westmoreland County in the Northern Neck. Thomas Ludwell, Richard Henry, Francis Lightfoot, William, and Arthur—each of these five men played impressive roles in the founding of this nation. President John Adams wrote of them, "that band of brothers, intrepid and unchangeable, who stood in the gap, in defense of their country, from the first glimmering of the Revolution in the horizon, through all its rising light, to its perfect day."

Richard Henry Lee may have been the most luminous of those five rising lights. He was born in 1732 and died in 1794. In those 62 years, some of the most turbulent in our history, his accomplishments were stunning. As a member of Virginia's House of Burgesses, Richard Henry's first bill is unique for that time: "To lay so heavy a duty on the importation of slaves as to put an end to that iniquitous and disgraceful traffic within the colony of Virginia."

"Africans," he wrote, were "equally entitled to liberty and freedom by the great law of nature." Imagine those words spoken in 1759. Is it any wonder they have been called "the most extreme anti-slavery statements made before the nineteenth century"? He was known as a blazing orator, so blazing that one of his admirers wrote, "I sometimes fancy that I was listening to some being inspired with more than mortal powers." Adding to the drama of his words, he would use his hands for emphasis, his right hand always wrapped in black silk because of a hunting accident. Enemies he had aplenty; at one point he was "outlawed" by a proclamation of English Governor Dunmore. In 1766, in response to the notorious Stamp Act, he coauthored the Leedstown Resolves. That's the one promising "danger and disgrace" to anyone who paid the tax because, "by reason and law he cannot be taxed but by consent of a Parliament, in which he is represented by persons chosen by the people."

In 1773 he proposed his celebrated plan for the formation of a "committee of correspondence" to keep the colonies informed about what was going on in Great Britain pertaining to the colonies in order to "form a closer union of the men of influence in each. And to kindle the flame of liberty, by spreading more widely correct information."

He was so highly regarded that his fellow delegates gave him the honor to "propose, on June 7, 1776, that the Continental Congress declare independence from Great Britain." Richard Henry Lee, delegate from Virginia, born in the Northern Neck.

Francis Lightfoot Lee

The "sweetest of all the Lee race" was how his niece described him, with a temper "as soft as the doves...." The man was Uncle Frank, Francis Lightfoot Lee, one of the Lee boys, those fabulous patriots that President John Adams called "that band of brothers."

While Richard Henry Lee may be the better known of all those Northern Neck-born shining lights, Francis Lightfoot is the more unsung. He was his brother Richard's opposite. Where Richard was the burning orator, sometimes dramatic, even flamboyant, Francis was quiet and self-effacing. He married Rebecca Tayloe for love, which was a bit unusual in those days when marrying to combine New World dynasties was more common. She was sixteen years old at the time of their wedding, and their letters to each other were said to be filled with much affection. To his dismay, he was away a lot. He was far more content to be at home at Menokin on the Northern Neck, with his books and his farm and his beloved wife, Becky. He was a good friend of Patrick Henry's, and was himself considered a radical. He was a signer of both the Westmoreland Resolves in 1766 and the Declaration of Independence in 1776. He served in the Virginia House of Burgesses; he was in Philadelphia in 1776 as a Virginia delegate to the second Continental Congress. Since all this activity represented much separation from his adored wife, where were their letters to each other? I haven't yet been able to find any, but I've found something else.

It's an essay about the man whom friends called Frank, an essay by Mark Twain. The thrust of the essay was, to quote Mark Twain, "to show what sort of material was used in the construction of congressmen in his day; since to sketch him is to sketch the average congressman of his time." After writing a bit of his family line, Twain writes,

> He dealt in no shams; he had no ostentations of dress or equipage.... He loved books; he had a good library, and no place had so great a charm for him as that. Over their port and walnuts, he and his friends of the gentry discussed a literature, which is dead and forgotten now, and political matters which were drowsy with the absence of corruption and "investigations." In short, Francis Lightfoot Lee was a gentleman—a word which meant a great deal in his day, though it means nothing whatever in ours. Mr. Lee defiled himself with no juggling, or wire pulling, or begging, to acquire a place in the provincial legislature, but went thither when he was called, and went reluctantly. He wrought there industriously during four years, never seeking his own ends, but only the public's. His course was purity itself, and he retired unblemished when his work was done. He retired gladly, and sought his home and its superior allurements. No one dreamed of such a thing as 'investigating' him.

Well, in times of political turbulence, it's good to look back at those words, so thank you, Mark Twain, and thank you, Frank Lee, one of the most ordinary and most extraordinary patriots of the Northern Neck.

The Blue Coat School

W hat possible relationship could an English school for impoverished children and orphans have with the Northern Neck? Well, imagine the great Virginia plantation owners of the eighteenth century in need of labor and an English school, founded and funded by a slave ship owner, turning out youngsters who could read, write and "do accounts." Many of these newly literate orphans were sold and sent to the New World as indentured servants, sometimes on ships carrying slaves. A match made in…? Well, certainly not heaven.

What happened to those youngsters when their service was completed? Did they try to return home to England? Traces of most of them have indeed been lost to history, but there are exceptions, Robert Biscoe being one of them, and he was quite an exception. I learned about him in the Christ Church Foundation's book, *People in Profile*, researched by Foundation volunteers. It details the lives of some of the folks living in Christ Church parish in Lancaster County from 1720 to 1750.

Biscoe was apparently sold to the wealthiest of all the planters in Lancaster County and beyond. It's likely the ship carrying Biscoe and others landed at Robert "King" Carter's dock in Lancaster County. Biscoe would have been about fourteen. He had spent four years at Blondell's Christ's Hospital—not a hospital at all, but the school known as the Blue Coat School—

in Liverpool. In its earliest days, the school was said to be a source for literate laborers who could be sold and sent wherever they were needed, particularly to the colonies. Biscoe would have worn a uniform for those four years—a blue coat, thus the school's nickname. Why blue? It was the Tudor color of alms giving and charity.

As an indentured servant, Robert Biscoe worked for Carter, doing his bookkeeping, even becoming a confidant of sorts. It's not clear why he was so highly regarded, but he must have been. One year before his seven-year service ended, he and a buddy, another indentured servant, stole some hogsheads of tobacco and went off, most likely to start their own merchant business. It was a short-lived adventure. He was captured and brought back to the Carter plantation, but his punishment was unusually light: an additional year of service to Carter.

When he was finally a free man, he did become a bona fide merchant, and along the way, he married into a prominent family, purchased land, and yes, he employed both indentured servants and a slave or two. And, he wrote and had published an astonishing little book about ledger keeping and currency, apparently of use to other merchants. This unusual talent can certainly be attributed to his education at the Blue Coat School.

Amazingly, (to me) the Blue Coat School and many sister blue coat schools are still going strong as boarding schools for boys and girls in England and the schools are said to be known for the quality education they provide to thousands of young people. It's nice to think that perhaps some of them have found their way, as free and curious travelers, to a very different Northern Neck.

James Madison's Trash...and Mine

Awhile back, I read a newspaper article that got me thinking, really seriously, about privacy. Not just any kind of privacy, but the privacy that respects the sanctity of, well, me and my trash, and your trash, and the trash belonging to famous people. Is all trash created equally liable to history snoops? This line of thought was sparked by the discovery of a huge so-called treasure trove of trash belonging to one of the most famous of the Northern Neck native sons, James Madison.

The trash discovery was made during the twenty-four-million-dollar restoration of Madison's estate at Montpelier. Matthew Reeves is Director of Archaeology for the Montpelier Foundation. He has been quoted as verifying that one hundred percent of the items we're finding were "being used by James and Dolly Madison in their daily lives." Michael Quinn, president of the foundation, has said, "We have found the mother lode."

This, about a man, a shy man, a modest man whom we know as the Father of our Constitution.

So what have they found in Madison's trash? Well, a fragment of a plate that probably dates back to Marie Antoinette. Well, he had friends in high places. A rib bone! So what does that tell us about Dolly and James? Hmmm. I guess they liked good cuts of beef. Shards from champagne bottles and engraved glasses: well, they had champagne tastes. Can we infer from this that

that's why the estate was deeply in debt when Madison died? That is, as my grandmother might have said, "champagne taste and a beer pocket."

I wonder if we are clutching at straws, or rib bones, because so little written material, particularly letters between the president and his first lady, have been found giving us tidbits about the personal lives of Dolly and James. The main reason for this dearth of letters was that they were so seldom apart that there was no need for writing notes to each other. Our loss, or their effort at privacy.

Other artifacts have been found in the midden—that is, the big trash pile. An article on the discovery explains, "Charred wood fragments, probably from fireplace used for cooking, have been salvaged and can be screened for seeds, egg shells and fish bones to learn more about Madison's diet."

Well, I think I've got to draw a line in the sand here. If my trash were exhumed, what would anyone learn about me through my diet? Oh dear! Shards from wine bottles, yes, but not champagne; more likely "Three Buck Chuck" wine and lots of tuna fish cans. Did the woman have a cat or a fish fetish? Crab shells and oyster shells—they found some of those at Montpelier. We Northern Neckers have a few things in common, perhaps including a bit of righteous indignation when it comes to garbage hunters!

Pirates!

Centuries ago, the Northern Neck had a rather special kind of tourist: pirates. Now, whether your first encounter with pirates was *Treasure Island,* watching a swashbuckling Errol Flynn movie, or, most recently, watching Johnny Depp try his hand at buccaneering, pirates, no matter how awful their deeds, have always been a source of fabulous and somewhat romanticized tales. There have always been pirates, or at least, as long as there have been ships carrying treasure there have been folks ready to thieve.

Here in the Northern Neck, it's reported that pirates arrived in the area around the time of the first settlers for the unbeatable shelter it provided. There were different varieties of pirates. The difference between a pirate and a privateer is that pirates did their thing illegally while privateers did the exact same things, but with the approval of their particular government. English privateers, like Capt. Kidd, carried a document called a "letter of marque," giving them royal authority to harass the shipping of England's enemies, the Spanish or French. It was essentially a license to steal. Kidd received his letter of mark from Charles the Second, and, when Kidd, he of the golden necklaces and toothpick, was successful, the king received, of course, a kingly share. The captain and crew received the balance, but without this letter of mark the plunderer was a pirate.

Forts were built here on the Neck to serve as lookouts

for the pirate ships. They were built on the Corrotoman and Rappahannock rivers and one near the great Wicomico, but they weren't very successful in keeping the pirates away from the richly loaded ships heading toward England. Guard ships proved far more effective, acting as convoys, staying with the merchant ships until they reached a so-called "safe riding place." Even so, Capt. Kidd, mad, mad Blackbeard and others were pretty successful, plying their dastardly trade right here on the Northern Neck.

The most famous pirate of all was a man generally unknown for piracy, our very own Capt. John Smith. According to one of his memoirs, as a young man, he sailed to Rome with a shipload of French and Spanish pilgrims. A great storm arose, and the pilgrims, believing him to be the cause of the storm, since he was an "enemy Englishman," threw him overboard. But our John swam to a nearby island, was rescued by pirate Capt. De La Roche, and then joined him, perhaps in gratitude, in a short spate of piracy. Happily for us, Capt. Smith was not a plunderer at heart, but was one of our greatest adventurers, famous for being the first Englishman to set foot on the Neck, to map the Neck, some say to discover the Neck. Thanks, Capt. Smith, so glad you sowed your wild oats elsewhere.

Gone Fishin'

The day I went to a favorite shop only to be greeted with a sign on the door proclaiming "gone fishing" was, well, memorable. My first reaction was disappointment. Then I was somewhat awed that what I thought of as recreation could take precedence over business. How little I knew about fishing fever on the Northern Neck, especially when it's rockfish season. But from sea bass to tilefish to flounder and crappie, every season there's fishing madness going on. All along the scores of creeks on the Neck, docks are festooned with everything from tiny rowboats to great sail and powerboats, waiting for the right moments, the right tide, to cast off for a few hours of fishing adventure on the rivers or the Bay.

Then I learned about another kind of fishing adventure, the kind of fishing called the most dangerous occupation in the world—commercial fishing—and I learned about it from a man who lives part time on the Neck, part time in Baltimore; a man whose books you may have read, William McCloskey. We met in the local coffee house, and talked about his newest book, *Raiders*, the third in his fictional trilogy, which vividly depicts the fishing industry. He is also the author of the acclaimed non-fiction account of the fishing industry, *Their Father's Work*.

How did a retired member of the Johns Hopkins University applied physics laboratory develop a passion for commercial fishing? Well, he was also a Coast Guard officer, a merchant

41

seaman, and a reporter for *The Baltimore Sun*.

He began hiring out on fishing boats during sabbaticals and vacations more than twenty-five years ago. He's fished with first and third world crews of many nationalities. *Kirkus Reviews* notes that he has fished for king crab in the Bering Sea in winter, when the crabs are at their plumpest and the sea its nastiest; he experienced the industrial-scale sardine fishery of Chile and the artisan fishing of Indonesia from small wooden boats. He's spent a good amount of time with the Japanese fleet. And he has served on patrol boats enforcing compliance with the welter of maritime laws. Reviewers have called his books "a splendid, subtle portrait of the fisherman." An old-time fisherman said to Bill McCloskey, "It's a livin', by, but it ain't much of a life now, is it?"

Reading Bill McCloskey's books, learning about the everyday lives of the men who hunt the seas for whales or sardines or halibut large enough to break a man's arm, gives new meaning to "gone fishing," even here, on the Northern Neck.

Watermen, Heroes of the Bay

It's been said that Virginia colonists, fishing the waters surrounding them, began calling themselves "watermen" after the men who worked the Thames River in England, and that the term "waterman" is only used on the Chesapeake Bay and the Thames.

Actually, those early London watermen weren't fishermen at all. The term "waterman" dates as far back as the eleventh century in England. These early English watermen went fishing all right, not for the bounty of the sea, but the booty: gold, silver, anything they could capture. In other words, they were pirates. Just as the highwaymen in not-so-merry old England were road robbers, watermen were sea robbers.

Of course, our very first watermen (as we refer to them today) in the New World were our Native Americans, working from their dugout canoes. And their catches were not so unlike today's haul of fish, eel and oysters, crabs and clams. Today's watermen still start their day at sunrise just as their ancestors did, working not from dugouts, but, depending on what era we're talking about, from a schooner, deadrise or bugeye, a shallop, a skipjack, buyboat, even a tug boat or push boat. Here on the Northern Neck, watermen and waterwomen remain heroes of the sea. Most are independent fishermen who own their boats and sell their catch to local wholesalers, carrying on the work of parents and grandparents and great great grandparents.

Back to the boats. Those watermen from earlier generations may have worked on schooners, sailing ships with at least two masts. The word "schooner" derives from the term "schoon/scoon," meaning to move smoothly and quickly. So smoothly and quickly that the author Joseph Conrad called them "birds of the sea whose swimming is like flying, and resembles more a natural function than a handling of manmade appliances." Another two-masted ship was the bugeye, and I've learned that's a flat-bottomed sailboat having sharply raked masts. It's a classic boat typical of the Chesapeake, where it was used frequently as a clam and oyster boat, and performed dredging while under sail. It was considered the quintessential oystering boat of the 1870s. Now what about the skipjack? Well, it's smaller than a schooner, with only one mast, and it became popular and dominated the oystering industry because it required fewer crewmen, and was less costly, both to build and maintain.

The waterman's tools for oystering, fishing, and crabbing run from the primitive to the somewhat sophisticated. No longer do they use wooden spears, but tongs, pound nets, line trawls, traps and hooks, lures, weights and sinkers are the tools of choice.

Here in the Northern Neck, like in many maritime communities, there are watermen traditions to maintain. Every May in Reedville, there is the blessing of the fleet. Local clergymen bless boats and their crews as they pass by in a procession. And of course the annual seafood festival held at Belle Isle State Park is not to be missed. There's the season for shad planking, and Kilmarnock has its crab festival, replete with crab races, lots of music and, of course, there are oyster roasts, oyster shucking contests and even local chefs competing for the she-crab soup crown—though the crown really belongs to those men and women, carrying on old traditions, tonguing for oysters, capturing crabs, fishing for shad, here, on the Northern Neck.

The Floating Theater

The Northern Neck is often called "rivah country," and it is, but it's also Bay and creek country, home to all things that float, even a bank. That was a while ago when a local bank launched a "bank 'n' boat" branch anchored at a wharf on Carters Creek. It was less than a success, since the watermen, I have been told by a former banker, didn't like the thought of their money sailing away.

But much earlier, the Wharf was home to an enormous success, though one preacher said, "The devil couldn't reach us by land so he's coming by water." The so-called devil was in the form of *The Captain James Adams Floating Theater*, and even the preachers came to love it. There are lots of older residents here who remember the thrill when the salt-water showboat arrived. Of course, Carters Creek wasn't its only port of call. From 1914 to 1941, it roamed the Bay area to ports in Maryland, Virginia and beyond the Bay to North Carolina. Theater historians tell us that it was an important cultural event for people in rural and small coastal towns. But how cultural is the question. It was live theater, and usually the only live theater some folks would ever see. From *Ten Nights in a Barroom* to *Over the Hill to the Poorhouse*, these were "hiss the villain, cheer the hero, weep for the heroine" tearjerkers. Charles Hunter, who was stage director as well as actor, was quoted as saying, "Villains and villainesses are necessary, for how could virtue triumph if there wasn't something wicked over which to triumph? But wickedness must be nice."

Hunter had his own real life drama on board. He was madly in love with Beulah Adams, sister of the floating theater's founder, James Adams; and against the wishes of big brother, they were eventually married. Beulah Adams was known as the Mary Pickford of the Chesapeake, and played ingénue roles well into her mid-life.

All of the actors portrayed stereotypical characters and variations in every play. They all lived on board this rather exotic barge, large enough to house the theatre and sleep and feed the entire company. It was 436 tons, 128.3 feet long and 34 feet wide, with an auditorium that could seat hundreds. It was the only showboat Edna Ferber visited to research her novel, *Show*. Jerome Kern and Oscar Hammerstein II also paid a visit before creating their musical based on the novel *Show Boat*.

Before James Adams got his idea for the floating theater, he and his wife had been partners in a circus aerial act. After trying a circus of his own, he toured the South with a small-time vaudeville show, and then, happily for theater history and rural America, he developed his dream for a floating playhouse. Long gone, it's still alive in the memories of many long-timers of the Northern Neck.

Steamboat Era Museum

C an you imagine a love affair lasting 150 years? Well, it really happened—the love affair between steamboats and the Northern Neck, and, of course, cities like Baltimore and Norfolk. It was the steamboat named *Patuxent* that in 1828 made its first run from Baltimore to the Northern Neck that began the great sea change in the life of the Northern Neck.

Folks would board the steamboat, perhaps from a wharf in Weems or Irvington, and embark on the great adventure that would take them to Baltimore for about a dollar. If you wanted the luxury of a private stateroom, it would cost you $1.50 extra. Hungry for breakfast after the excitement of waiting for the whistle of the steamboat sounding its arrival? No problem. For fifty cents, you could get a country breakfast in the posh dining room. Lunch was seventy-five cents, and dinner one dollar. If you were a newlywed, you'd probably upgrade from one of the many staterooms to one of the two bridal suites. Perhaps you would spend a weekend experiencing the sophisticated culture of the big city. Maybe you'd come home with sacks of oranges and other exotic stuff not then available on the Neck.

Folks from Baltimore would board for a different kind of exotica, because a trip to the Northern Neck would be made, not for the quiet charm and beauty that so often brings vacationers here today, but the chance to visit a luxury beachfront resort or go to the opera; perhaps to go roller skating at the rink or shop at very stylish shops.

Terri Thaxton is Executive Director of the Steamboat Era Museum in Irvington. She said, "People came and spent weeks at a time here. Most people would think that in the middle of nowhere there would be nothing happening except some people fishing and farming, but there was a lot going on."

The steamboat era did come to an end in the 1930s. What happened and how it happened is beautifully documented at the Steamboat Era Museum in Irvington. It's a wonderful place to learn about those golden days. Terri Thaxton told us about the museum's oral history center, where stories told by eyewitnesses to that era are recorded and then integrated with photo exhibits. The museum's "Ships and Sailors" section is chock full of information with dioramas, sketches and photos depicting both the Union and Confederacy with "The Bay At War." It documents the time from 1861 to 1865 when the Chesapeake became the focus of attention for gunboats, smugglers, privateers, shoreline artillery fire, tidewater guerrillas and blockade-running oystermen.

The museum's mission statement says it all: "The Steamboat Era Museum is a memorial to a romantic and entrepreneurial time that helped broaden our horizons and shape our world." Their motto is, "We are who we are because steamboats were," and those memories come alive at the Steamboat Era Museum, right here on the Northern Neck.

Menhaden, the Inedible Fish

Imagine being surrounded by hundreds of thousands of pounds of fish, fish of such a special species that not a one is fit to eat unless you're a bluefish or a shark, or seriously starving. They're menhaden fish, an oily, smelly, bony fish not suitable for the efforts of even the most adventurous cook, but your pets will love them when they're processed into pet food. Other fish love them, too, so they're a great baitfish, and they're supposed to be good for you when they become fish oil supplements. Fertilizer made from menhaden is terrific for your garden. The early colonists stubbornly refused the Indians' suggestion to use the fish to increase the yield of their crops. Must have been the smell.

Millions and millions of pounds of them are caught in the waters off the Neck, much processed in factories in Reedville, a town at the tip of the Neck named for Capt. Elijah Reed, who sailed into Cockerell's Creek in 1867 with two ships equipped with giant kettles. The first factory ships in this area, they "caught 'em and cooked 'em" right there in the waters of Cockerell Creek.

Menhaden is big business in the Neck. Smelly business, say those living downwind who can, on a good day, or rather, a bad day, take in the profitable aroma of the menhaden industry. Besides the occasional whiff, there are the sounds that remind us of this major Neck industry: the sounds of the small spotter planes circling the waters to alert the fishing boat captains and their fleet to menhaden sightings. Such tame game hunting sounds aren't exactly out of a macho Hemingway novel, but they are part of a so far unchanging way of life that keeps the Northern Neck uncommonly stable in a less-than-stable world.

Chantey Singers

Perhaps you've read about, or even heard, the kind of sea chanteys sung by the crews of nineteenth century American and British sailing ships, but have you ever heard of menhaden chanteys—chanteys that are a legacy of African-American work songs, sung on the water; adaptations of the work songs sung while lumbering, mining, building roads and levees, and, yes, picking cotton. They were a way, sometimes the only way, of gaining control over the pace of their work.

The so-called menhaden chanteys are being kept alive by an awe-inspiring group of men, the Northern Neck Chantey Singers, all of whom have retired from the backbreaking work of hauling up nets laden with thousands of pounds of menhaden. William Hudnall organized the groups in 1991 at the request of the Greater Reedville Association. Just to orient you, Reedville is at the tip of the Northern Neck and was known as the menhaden capital of the world. Hudnall wasn't sure he would find men who would be willing to sing these chanteys for the public, so he was delighted when he found thirteen volunteers, all retired African-American watermen from Northumberland County who worked in the menhaden fishery for over a fifty-year period, beginning in the 1930s for the oldest of them and the 1980s for some of the younger men. All of them did their share of pulling and singing on the water. Sometimes there were as many as forty men on each of the long rowboats, pulling in the nets and singing.

The singing wasn't done out of joyousness or thankfulness, but need. The rhythm of the songs coordinated the efforts of hauling in the nets to bring the fish to the surface, where they could then be transferred to the hold of the mother ship.

So how can a simple melody help bring in these terrible loads? William Hudnall says, "The harmony brings everybody together on the same chord at the same time and that's what made the work easier." Hudnall describes the effect of the chanteys: "You'd be straining, and you'd be pulling as hard as you possibly could pull, and I mean you'd be straining, and you couldn't get the fish to come up at all. Then somebody hit that chantey, and started to get into it, and after a while, it starts coming up, inch by inch, after a while they'd start showing."

The group has a CD called *See You When the Sun Goes Down*. They've performed in Virginia and Maryland, with requests coming in from all over the country. Lavernia George of the Smithsonian said, "The original sources of these songs are dying out, so it's more important than ever to preserve them." Well, our very own Northern Neck Chantey Singers are doing just that. Thank you, gentlemen.

John Smith's Barge

Imagine sixty-three volunteers, men and women, working more than 4,000 hours to recreate something they had never seen. Well, it happened here on the Northern Neck, in the Reedville Fishermen's Museum boat shop, to be exact. The aim was to recreate the barge used by Capt. John Smith and perhaps a dozen Jamestown crew men to chart and explore, for the first time ever, the great Chesapeake Bay and its creeks. The result: *The Spirit of 1608*, a barge, or for accuracy's sake, a shallop.

It was built with "best guess" accuracy because no plans or even useful descriptions exist. That doesn't mean it was done without enormous vigorous historical research, including combing through Smith's own diaries and papers for clues. One small clue from his diary was this quote: "Being in an open barge of near three tons burden." Other accounts provided hints as to the interior space, the draft, the mast, the sail and oars. I've read that historians still disagree on some design details, but Chuck Backus, Executive Director of the Reedville Fishermen's Museum, says that their re-creation represents their best interpretation of clues based on solid historical research.

To give you some idea of the research efforts, Stuart Hopkins, a professional sail maker and the volunteer who crafted the sails, wrote, "The boat shop guys wanted a tanbark sail for effect, but weren't sure it would be historically correct until we stumbled on this circa 1600s Dutch painting from the collection at the National Maritime Museum, in Greenwich, England, a view full of wonderful detail. It not only authorized the use of a tanbark cloth, but served as inspiration as we made the sails."

The iron fittings were researched and then forged by volunteers from the Blacksmith Guild of Hughlett Tavern in Heathsville, another town on the Neck filled with signs of the early history of the Neck.

The wood for the shallop came from ancient white oak trees that were victims of the 2003 hurricane, Isabel. The enormous pieces were gathered by the volunteers, and labored over in the woodworking shop of the museum, to become the planks of the little craft. Chuck Backus is still awed by the volunteers' dedication. "A hurricane comes through, devastates the place, and our volunteers turn it into something incredibly positive."

In the end, the extraordinary result: a charming ancient-looking twenty-eight-foot barge, *The Spirit of 1608*. The "little barge that could" has been featured in the PBS documentary series *Nova* and made an appearance at the 2007 National Folklife Festival in Washington, D.C.

I wonder if Capt. John Smith and his Jamestown crew would have felt at home in this labor of love and dedication to history. Capt. Smith referred to his shallop as "the discovery barge." There are at least sixty-three people here on the Northern Neck looking forward to having thousands and thousands of folks rediscovering how much began here, on the Northern Neck of Virginia.

Fish Spotters

How is it possible to spot small fish in a huge body of water from a small plane flying some thousands of feet above? Easy, if the fish are menhaden, that oily, bony, inedible fish. They swim in enormous schools and darken the waters wherever they are. Sometimes the school's so big, the water looks as if moving islands have sprung up; but there is no moveable island, rather, a moveable feast for bluefish and other species that feed on menhaden; and a moveable quarry for the menhaden fishing boat fleets.

Spotting that quarry is the job, not surprisingly, of the fish spotters, flying over the waters. If we're talking about the Northern Neck, and we are, the "waters" are the waters of the Chesapeake Bay. In other parts of the country and the world, fish spotter pilots are on the lookout over the oceans and seas for everything from whales to tuna and herring. Here on the Neck, it's menhaden.

The story goes that following World War II, a barnstorming pilot was flying over Reedville, the home of the menhaden industry, taking visitors on an aerial tour of the town. He was redirected to look for schools of menhaden, and then to contact the fishing boat captains below him as to their whereabouts. This, so it is said, was the beginning of the aerial fish spotter profession here.

Fish spotting, but not quite from the height of a small plane, used to be the job of sailors, scurrying up to the crow's nest of his ship, on the lookout for fish. The Northern Neck's very first fish spotter was our explorer and adventurer, John Smith. He records in his journal in 1607 that he sailed across the Chesapeake Bay through schools of fish, "lying so thick with their heads above the water, as for want of nets (our barge driving amongst them) we attempted to catch them with a frying pan."

Today, no frying pan to catch menhaden and cook them in your kitchen is recommended. Those slippery fish are valuable for many things, from fish oil to fertilizer, but dreadful to eat, no matter your culinary skills.

Today, the spotter pilots contact the captains by radio to direct the mother ships to their prey, then forty-foot-long boats are deployed with giant nets. The nets are cast out, and very soon are closed up, filled with thousands of fish, then transported to the refrigerated holds of the big ships, then on to the processing plants.

The spotter pilots have been called our eyes in the skies. In other parts of the world, they are on the lookout, maybe for tuna for your next sushi roll, or working with scientists, collecting information for a wide variety of research projects. Here, on the Northern Neck, it's menhaden they're on the lookout for, perhaps not "lying so thick," but still thick enough to sustain a major industry.

Community Newspapers

Small-town newspapers are often the heartbeat of the community they serve, bringing local news, features, and opinions to everyone who cares to read them, and nearly everyone does in the Northern Neck of Virginia. Perhaps because of its history of isolation, the newspapers here play an outsized role in the life of the Neck.

As a little orientation, the Northern Neck is a skinny body of land sitting between the Rappahannock and Potomac rivers on the Chesapeake Bay. It's known for its hundreds of lovely hidden creeks and wooded landscapes. When Capt. John Smith left Jamestown to go exploring, just about four hundred years ago, and first saw the Northern Neck, he was reported to have written in his notebook, "Heaven and earth never agreed better to frame a place for man's habitation." Well, isolation put a brake on habitation, at least serious habitation, for quite a while. Because of its isolation, steamboats were a lifeline, traveling back and forth from Baltimore to the many wharfs and docks on the Neck, carrying everything from news and wagon parts to brides.

Then, in the mid 1900s, two bridges were built linking the Neck to the big cities like Richmond and beyond. But before that, and since, local newspapers have been a very special kind of bridge, going straight into the heart of the community, with articles about local politics; the wildlife column telling us

57

there's definitely been an eagle sighting; the articles, sometimes salted ever so lightly, with gossip about local folks writing best sellers and not-so-best sellers; and news about who was going to be the speaker at the local DAR meeting, about which of our students won scholarships and about who had gone to war in Iraq; letters to the editors from folks worrying about the new folks in town known as come-here's, with strange ideas and tastes. The unwritten message in some of those letters: a pox upon the bridges.

The newspapers' editors are a bit unique, one taking leave to do some heavy-duty farming on land his family owned for generations, another writing the definitive book on deadrises. Then there is that funny expectation that if it's not in the local paper, it just may not be worth talking about. The talking about takes place, of course, in the local barbershop. No man is safe from a short interrogation session after getting a haircut. How do they really feel about the article on the new vineyard or who will win the seat on the school board?

The early colonists needed news as much as we; their first paper was called *The Public Occurrences*. It came out in 1665, and you know what? Public occurrences haven't changed that much. We still read the obits and the church news, and we've learned long ago to sift gossip from fact, and sometimes we prefer the former to the latter. I understand Capt. John Smith had the same problem.

The Little Theater That Could

E very couple of years, the magazine published by the Northern Neck Electric Cooperative, a magazine mailed to more than 350,000 readers, conducts what they call The Delightful Dozen contest, asking readers all across Virginia to submit their favorite choices for the "best of" in twelve categories. One of those categories was "community theater," and from the scores of community theaters in Virginia, the Westmoreland Players came up the winner. How and why did this "little theater that could" in Callao, Virginia come out on top?

Well, for starters, they have a devoted core of volunteers. Many have been Players since its very beginnings, in 1979, when they lived the life of gypsy performers, putting on plays wherever there was a large enough performance space; plays that ranged from Shakespeare to the most modern. All had outstanding production values, including sets that were very nearly professional looking.

And then, in 2000, after years of this nomadic but highly successful life, the dream of all community theaters came true: a home of their own. One of their performance spaces, a kind of event center, was for sale, and after much consideration, and even more fundraising, the membership took the plunge. They bought the building, and then performed their greatest hit. They transformed a ho-hum space into a real playhouse, and now they were, literally, in business.

But that presented difficult decisions: could they afford to put on plays that might be financially unsuccessful? Perhaps not, so play selections have a new dimension. But their range of productions remains impressive. Maybe they won't put on *Waiting for Godot*, but their stunning productions of the classic *To Kill a Mockingbird* and of *The Importance of Being Earnest* are mighty good.

Glen and Joy Evans have been a guiding force that has helped shepherd the Players to the top. The roles they have played since 1996 with the Westmoreland Players include that of artistic director, producer, play selectors, teachers, coaches, even costume designer. In a parallel life, since 1993, Joy and Glen have been involved with the Maryland Renaissance Festival as actors, directors, and teachers. With the Players, they are quick to say that they are only part of the force behind the their success; they were already doing outstanding community theater before their arrival and there is a strong board of directors, an amazing pool of talent, coming from all over the Northern Neck and beyond, and an appreciative audience that fills the house at almost every performance.

Nancy Royall is a long-time member, and she told me, "My love for this theater is really associated with our ability to promote that sense of community and wonder that we get watching our neighbors on the stage."

Glen and Joy share their vision for the group with all the working members of the Westmoreland Players: "To keep growing, and yes, aspire to greatness." Why not? After all, they're the little theater that could, right here in the Northern Neck.

Bloom Where You're Planted

A man I hugely admire remarked to me a while back, "Bloom where you're planted." He didn't say it as advice, or as an imperative, but just as a simple matter of fact. It was what he had done in his lifetime, throughout all the ages and stages of his life thus far.

I had never heard the phrase before, but it certainly got me thinking about some of the people I've known or heard about, here on the Northern Neck of Virginia, where for some, I'm sure, blooming came harder than to others.

I'm thinking of one of the very first black menhaden fishing boat captains, Capt. Carroll Curry. I've not met him, but I have been told about some of the early hardships he endured. I know a couple of his brothers whom I would put in that "bloomer" category as well. One, Joe Curry, was also a menhaden fishing boat captain a long time ago, and today has a kind of pottery empire, with concrete lawn ornaments sprouting on his large lot in Kilmarnock. There you can find everything from lighthouses and windmills to ducks and dogs and turtles and herons. It's hard to find a "do good" organization on the Neck without Joe Curry's name on the board of directors. He's won lots of awards for his tireless work with the Northern Neck free health clinic.

"Bloom where you're planted." For so many people, it seems it's just in their genes, it appears so effortless. It's just what you do, one of my bloomers told me. I decided to look up the phrase, and after a Google second or two, I was stunned to find scores of sites headed with those words. Then came a torrent of sites offering books, catalogs, calendars, cards, posters, aprons, tea towels, recipes, wall hangings, and anything you can possibly think of that can be embellished with a few words, and some things I hope you won't think of.

So, did that corrupt for me, the real truth behind the phrase? Not really, not when I think of a recently transplanted Northern Necker, who was widowed shortly after she and her husband had built their dream home. She is volunteering and working, growing along with the blooming.

Then there is a woman who perhaps most exemplifies the phrase: Sharon Baldacci, who has had multiple sclerosis for more than twenty years, and is a recently published author. It runs in the family: her brother is best-selling author David Baldacci. Her fictionalized account of her life—Sundog Moment, about living, coping and growing with MS—is filled with hope and the sunshine needed for blooming. Many believe there is a wondrous abundance of that kind of sunshine, right here on the Northern Neck.

Divine Wine

They produced it, drank it and loved it in 1609; some swear to have proof they did it in 1607; Thomas Jefferson couldn't live without it and advised everyone else to imbibe, including a number of presidents before and after him. Yes, it's wine. Not French wine, or Italian, South African or Australian, but Virginia wine, and from grapes grown on Virginia soil. It is an established industry and growing, and I learned that Virginia is the fifth largest producer of wine in this country from the owner of a vineyard I visited while touring the tiny island of Malta, an island easy to fall in love with.

During some conversation with the owner of the winery, he asked where I was from, and when I told him, he extolled the virtues of Virginia wines, but he had never heard of the wineries of the Northern Neck, or of the Northern Neck. I tried to draw some comparisons, probably faulty, with Malta, to the climate and soil of the Northern Neck. I told him about the Northern Neck wine trail, where, with wine trail map in hand, you can go from one to another of our wineries, wine tasting your way across the Neck, which he thought would be a great idea for Malta, with a surprising number of vineyards for such a very small country.

I told him what I knew about the Neck's wineries. I told him about Athena, in Burgess, one of the newest. It was the dream of three retired healthcare workers who really believed in its health benefits. When I told him about Belle Mount vineyards near Warsaw, the name of that town took some explaining to the Maltese gentleman. I told him a bit about award-winning Ingleside Vineyards near Oak Grove, and about Oak Crest Vineyard in King George (more explaining to my Maltese friend) and White Fences Vineyard & Winery, another new addition. It's in Irvington and it is home to the infamous fall grape stomp. My host definitely knew about grape stomping; after all, wine has played an important role in the culture of the Mediterranean countries for thousands of years.

Wine has played a role in Virginia culture for only 399 years—as of the date when I parted with the Maltese winemaker, which I did most reluctantly.

He and his wife promised to check out the wineries of the Northern Neck the next time they came to the States. It was a lovely encounter, with wine bridging the seas, from the Mediterranean all the way to the Northern Neck.

Farming, a Family Affair

Some time ago, I was invited to interview a group of farmers whose collective years of farming would easily come to well over six hundred years. The men were wise, it seemed to me, and funny, and philosophical about the future of farming in the Northern Neck. Some thought it was inevitable that their children would not want to continue farming, and others were just as sure that their children would stay on after they were gone. The interviews were filmed, and one day, after some prodigious cutting, will be shown at the new farm museum, a work in progress in the Northern Neck, built on land donated by Luther Welch, one of the farmers in the group I talked with.

As a follow up, I've been asked to interview their wives, alternately called by some the original desperate housewives, or farm wives, or farmers' wives. I can't wait to talk with them. I've already met some of the women on social occasions and I can tell you, nary a one is desperate, but I do have questions—lots—and the first I want to ask is, "Do you consider yourself a farmers' wife or a farmer?" Then I'd ask:

- What kept you on the farm when doors to other possible options were beginning to open?
- Why did you stay?
- Was it tough raising children?
- Do you think it's tougher raising kids on the farm than raising kids in a city?

- As a mother, sister, daughter, even granddaughter farmer, working the land of your ancestors, what stories do you want the farm museum to tell about your way of life, and the way of life of your family?
- Did you ever throw a frying pan at the rooster who crowed at 4 a.m.?
- Lots of things have been mechanized on the farm, but that rooster still crows. Do you miss any of the old ways of doing things that technology has relieved you of, like milking cows?
- Traditionally, your way of life has been the backbone of agriculture and, yes, the backbone of our community and thousands of communities all over this country. Now, developers are offering to buy up farmland. Do you feel that they are buying your way of life? They can't buy your past but do you worry that they are buying your future and the future of your children?
- Is it all bad, or could this be a good thing, or is it really some place in the middle?
- Could it be that we who consume what you grow have so romanticized the past, that we have forgotten to ask *you*?"

I can't wait to get their answers.

Women-Owned Businesses

Here in the Northern Neck, the tourism council touts its "trails and tours," for all to enjoy. There's the wine trail, the eco-tour, the antique trail, the farm tour, and the like. I propose a new tour: the women-owned businesses trail. Their numbers are extraordinary for a small area like the Northern Neck, and I'm not talking about the hobbyists, those wannabe shop owners who open late, close early and then really close! I'm talking about businesses that have been here for years. They range from dress shops (one has been in business for more that thirty years) to hair salons, pharmacies and farms, wineries, a sailing school, and a hardware store, to restaurants owned by highly trained chefs.

On the main road of shops in White Stone, ninety percent of the businesses are women-owned. So—why? Their numbers exceed the national average. Are there more female risk-takers, or could it be the Northern Neck's colonial heritage? After all, the area was discovered at about the same time as Jamestown, and in colonial days, women, in addition to their daily domestic work, were maids, cooks, laundresses and seamstresses, and more to the point, usually through inheritance, but not always, they owned businesses. Women owned apothecaries, foundries, taverns and print shops. They were barbers, midwives, sextons and blacksmiths.

But of course, not all the Neck's women business owners have their roots here. Maybe "here" is the operative word. Perhaps it's because, whether you are a come-here, a been-here or a come-back-here, you have the freedom, in this very unique corner of the world, to reinvent yourself. This place, which seems to speak tranquility and retirement, seems also to offer the opportunity for reinvention with a most generous spirit. Perhaps these women are saying, "No more working for someone else; no more school teaching or bookkeeping. I can do beekeeping or open a crab house, and if I haven't quite yet decided what I want to do with the rest of my life, whether I'm forty or fifty or sixty or yes, eighty or whatever, I have the feeling that I've found a place that gives me the space to wait it out."

The New Farm Museum

The history of the Neck runs deep in the history of the United States, and so much has been written about this area: past, present and future. Words, words, words. What about things, artifacts that bring history to life?

Well, we have lots of museums here for that, and now a new one is "a'bornin'." But it's a museum with a difference, a museum that will celebrate the past, present, and future. It's the Northern Neck's farm museum and its fancy and formal name is the Luther Welch Agricultural Center, named after a still-robust hearty sixth generation Northern Neck working farmer who has donated eight acres of his rich and fertile land for the project, with a building designed by historic Williamsburg architect William E. Gwilliam.

So, why a museum dedicated to farming when farming is alive and well and ongoing? Well, in truth, it ain't what it used to be. As an example, there used to be acres and acres of tomato farms, so many that the Neck had its own tomato canning factories. Today, the cans that held those delightful fruits are, well, memorabilia. Many large family farms have been sold to developers as farmer's children turn to other careers. On the other hand, there are still many working farms, some growing specialty crops using innovative farming techniques and tools.

Of course, that's where the museum will be able to link the past with the future. Mr. Welch and his wife Margaret look at their collection of one hundred years worth of farming equipment and tools and feel sure there's much to learn from them. Mr. Welch has said that with each crop there's a story as to how the machinery has changed, and changed farming. There is already a traveling exhibit of some of those antique farm tools that has toured the schools, and the museum will also save the stories of Northern Neck farming for future generations with oral histories and exhibits that will display the economic and social heritage of the family farm, going back to colonial days. There are plans for canning factory displays, milking stations, a windmill, and more.

We look forward to this celebration of Northern Neck farming with the planned museum building, petting farm, vegetable and flower gardens. Watch the cannery demonstrations, check out the sawmill and steam engines, then, we will begin to understand what's been so often said: the family farm is the foundation of who we are as a commonwealth.

Saving the Land, One Acre at a Time

Albert Schweitzer wrote, "Man has lost the capacity to foresee and to forestall. He will end by destroying the earth." Well, happily, not all men and women have lost the capacity to foresee and forestall. About five years ago, here in our small corner of the earth, the Northern Neck, a land conservancy group was started by some conservation-minded people who wanted to see the Northern Neck grow gracefully and retain its economically viable farms and forests.

Mary Louisa Pollard is the president of the Northern Neck Land Conservancy (NNLC). Remember, she said, "Everything that is done on the land affects the water and the quality of the water that surrounds us."

Their mission: "to preserve the rural heritage of the Northern Neck by conserving its lands, waters, economies and culture for future generations." They do this by helping land owners, many of whom have been good stewards of their family land for generations, learn how to protect their land with voluntary land preservation agreements, which permit them to keep their land, and even derive tax benefits.

Along with hundreds of other conservancy groups in this country, the Northern Neck Land Conservancy is organized as a charitable organization under federal tax laws. They can purchase land for permanent protection, or accept donations of land or the funds to purchase land, accept a bequest, or accept the donation of a conservation easement. An easement permanently limits the type and scope of development that can take place on the land. The Northern Neck group, only a few years old, has helped place easements on more than 4,500 acres of land in the Northern Neck.

Some of those acres belong to Luther and Margaret Welch. They donated a conservation easement totaling seventy-one acres of their farmland surrounding what one day will be the Northern Neck Farm Museum. Welch is a true believer in land conservancy. Why? He says he sees farmers selling off their land for development, and later, "They come back home and they have nothing: no land and no way to provide for their families. No way to grow their food or food for others."

Anne Carter is another Northern Neck resident who shares the conservancy's vision. She is a descendant of Nicolas George, who arrived in the Neck in 1659 with the rights to more than seven hundred acres of land in Lancaster County. One hundred and forty-five acres are left, Ann Carter's Lombardy Grove Farm. She recently enrolled the farm in an easement.

Kathryn Gregory is the chairman of NNLC's Heritage Land Preservation Committee. She says, "It is immensely rewarding to know that some of the beautiful farms, forests, and waterfront areas which so define the Northern Neck will be preserved so that they may be enjoyed in the future." Thank you, land conservationists, and our children and our children's children thank you.

The Queens of the Northern Neck

I learned about them through a chance meeting that can be best depicted by this imagined conversation, sounding a bit like "Jabberwocky" out of *Alice in Wonderland*: "The Russians are coming! The Italians too, and they're bringing their queens!"

What else could I think to ask but "Oh my, what am I going to wear?"

The response, of course: "White, you silly, that way they'll barely see you."

This conversation could actually have taken place with Lynn Kallus, a fledgling beekeeper, and of course that's where the queens come in. Lynn is one of the few—new or experienced—beekeepers on the Northern Neck. Why so few? The commercial farm crops here are pollinated by insects and the wind rather than by wild honeybees. Farmers in other areas of the country, dependent on the wild honeybees for pollination, are now paying beekeepers to set up hives to pollinate their crops, because the wild honeybee population has been seriously diminished by pesticides and the like.

My friend Lynn, in beekeeping parlance, is a hobbyist beekeeper, one who keeps fifty hives or less. She does aspire to full beekeeper-hood status, not for pollinating services, but for honey. I can almost see those jars of pure Northern Neck honey.

Lynn prefers Italian and Russian bees, the Italians for their gentleness and the Russians for their resistance to mites. And you needn't go to Russia or Italy for them. You order them from an aviary; they arrive via the U.S. Postal Service in a three-pound wooden box holding about ten thousand bees and, yes, a queen. The post office lets Lynn know the minute they arrive since a bee or two or three has been know to escape and go a' buzzin'.

Lynn has had a few setbacks. She recently lost two hives due to the death of a queen and the laziness of another. Amazingly, the bees who lost their queen simply joined other hives, and then Lynn firmly took charge of Queen Lazy by combining her hive with a productive one, thus creating a two-queen hive. Talk about Alice in Wonderland!

That's when I asked about proper beekeeping attire. Yes indeed, white from head to toe, because bees don't pay attention to white. But if you're wearing dark clothing and move quickly around the hives, honeybees just might associate you with a big, brown, honey-loving bear, and then, watch out!

We honey-loving Northern Neckers will be keeping an eye on Lynn. May her beehives increase and continue to give her as much pleasure as the thought of those jars of Northern Neck honey gives us.

Barleycorn

You probably haven't given much thought to barley lately. You'll learn why I have in a couple of moments.

Along with wheat, it was a staple cereal of ancient Egypt, where it was used to make bread and beer; together, these were a complete diet, at least long, long ago; the ritual significance of barley dates back to ancient Greece, and before.

Remember these words from Robert Burns' song about John Barleycorn?

> John Barleycorn was a hero bold,
> Of noble enterprise,
> For if you do but taste his blood,
> 'Twill make your courage rise.
> Then let us toast John Barleycorn,
> Each man a glass in hand;
> And may his great posterity
> Ne'er fail in old Scotland!

Of course, that's Robert Burns' famous ode to, well, John Barleycorn and whiskey. Hold on now, this really has something to do with the Northern Neck, where Robert Burns' birthday is celebrated with gusto (and I'm told, with John Barleycorn); but something else has been taking place in the Northern Neck for the last couple of years, and yes, it has to do with whiskey.

A new brand of Virginia whiskey called Wasmund Single Malt whiskey is being made from a very superior barley called Thoroughbred, a variety of winter barley released in 2003 by Virginia Tech's agricultural experiment stations, now grown right here in the Northern Neck by enterprising Heathsville farmer Billy Dawson. The whiskey part of this story started when a neophyte distiller, Rick Wasmund, created Copper Fox distillery in order to brew a single malt whiskey. He had gone to Scotland to intern at a Scottish brewery, learned all he could, and went on a search to find the essential ingredient he felt he needed to create a superior single malt whiskey: a superior strain of barley. After a good deal of research, he learned that the barley called Thoroughbred would be perfect for his "dream whiskey." The Virginia Crop Improvement Association referred Rick to Billy Dawson, and their passions for perfection meshed.

Billy Dawson, who had been farming since 1986, was growing Thoroughbred barley, and had always wanted to start a mill. He and a partner did, about a year ago. The work of milling is tedious and time consuming and not a lot of farmers want to do it. Though their most popular product is whole kernel corn, it's the barley that sets Billy Dawson's place apart from the ordinary mill. In order to keep the barley product pure—that is, to keep the seed identity of this special barley preserved—he had to take some unusual steps, like having his fields certified as only growing Thoroughbred, and insuring that the mill's filters and bins are carefully cleaned after processing other grains.

Dawson hauls about six tons of the cleaned and bagged barley at a time to Copper Fox Distillery, and hauling must be in dedicated containers to keep the barley uncontaminated by other grains. That's just the beginning. No wonder Billy Dawson and his partner stand pretty much alone in, well, a field of Thoroughbred barley. Right here in the Northern Neck.

Tomatoes

I've never given much thought to tomatoes. I've kind of taken them for granted—until I read the happy history of that round fruit, and its unhappy history here in the Northern Neck.

The happy part is that we eat them at all. When they were first brought to this country, it was thought they were a dangerous, and even poisonous fruit until, legend tells us, in 1820, a Col. Johnson changed that perception. No, he didn't employ serious scientific tests. Instead, it's been reported that he stood on the steps of the Salem, New Jersey courthouse and somehow ate an entire basket of that strange fruit. Why he did it has yet to be uncovered, but he was certainly a great and early P.R. man. He had publicized the event, and more than 2,000 incredulous folk watched, perhaps waiting for him to keel over. He did not, and that feat is supposed to have kick-started this country's love affair with the tomato.

Now, the rest of this story isn't legend; it's fact. Sometime in the 1880s, farmers in the Northern Neck discovered that the soil was perfect for growing especially delicious varieties of the now popular tomato, and that tomatoes could be processed and canned and still taste great. Canneries began to spring up, built on docks and wharves, a most sensible location, enabling equipment to be brought by ship directly from the factories. And of course, the processed tomatoes could then be packed and shipped, mostly to Baltimore. Cannery fever was contagious, and eventually there were about one hundred factories providing seasonal work, and in most cases, back-breaking work, for many hundreds of people: farmers and factory workers, planting, picking, hauling to the wooden shed factories; scalding, coring, peeling, packing; labeling by hand, "Wife's Pride," "Pride of Virginia," "Southern Leader."

There are many people here on the Neck who can remember parents and grandparents working on the farms, or in the canneries. In that era, many people were living at or near the poverty level, and this mostly summer work was a great boon for unskilled laborers, of which there were many, and great for teenagers. They could earn a few dollars, maybe for books, maybe for shoes. Everyone benefited, from farmer to factory owner, to the folks doing the nasty work.

And then, the end of an era began. No, it wasn't early warning about global warming, and there was no change in the fertile soil. World War II had come to an end. There was the advent of the big chain store buying all the tomatoes a farmer could produce, great for the farmer, not so great for the cannery owner, and at just about the same time, those factories were beginning to have trouble meeting modern health and safety standards. And then there was the labor pool—it was getting more and more difficult to find people willing to work in the fields, or to stand over steaming cauldrons of tomatoes. There were better jobs available now, jobs that would pay more than a few dollars a week.

What remains of the rosy era of Northern Neck tomatoes? If you hunt long enough in the local antique shops, you might be lucky enough to find old tomato crates, and quaint tomato can labels. But far better than that, and this is the happy part of the story, the soil is still great, and while there are large farms growing barley and wheat and corn, there are numerous small boutique farms growing every imaginable variety of tomato, from fat heritage and beefsteaks to tiny grape-sized ones. Our local farmers' markets and farm stands are filled with them, those especially delicious tomatoes, grown right here, on the Northern Neck.

Community-Supported Agriculture

The poet and farmer Wendell Berry observed, "How we eat, determines to a considerable extent, how the world is used...." In other words, the choices we make about the food we eat have far-reaching effects, effects that go way beyond our dinner tables. There is a very good chance that the vegetables you bought for tonight's dinner traveled 1,300 miles, from the farm to the supermarket, unless you grow all your own, buy your produce exclusively at a farmers' market or you are a member of a CSA farm.

CSA stands for community-supported agriculture, and that means people directly supporting small local farms, and receiving a share of the farmers' harvest. I learned about CSA's—there are about 1,700 in this country—while making a visit to the local farmers' market where meeting, greeting and eating are just a few of the joys of market days here on the Northern Neck.

Actually, I discovered CSA through my passion for fresh garlic. There, at one of the farm stands, was a box filled with fresh garlic. And still attached to the bulbs was something I had never seen before: thin, curled, green stalks. They're called garlic scapes and if you're a garlic fan and lucky enough to find them in early summer, the taste will be a joyous discovery. The folks manning and womanning the farm stand were John Cooper and his mom, owners of Olin-Fox Farms in Reedville. The banner on their stand said, "A CSA farm." After regaling me about garlic scapes, and giving me a bouquet of them, along with some great recipes, John told me they owned one of only two CSA farms on the Northern Neck.

The origin of CSA farms goes back about forty years. They were started in Japan by a group of women who were concerned about the decline of family farms and the huge increase of food imports. They made a deal with local farmers to link up with the community and develop something akin to family membership clubs, with families buying shares of seasonal crops.

John's Olin-Fox Farms, like all CSA farms, provide their members with in-season, fresh, high-quality vegetables. Theirs are all certified organic and when you pick up your weekly share, you receive an extra bonus: their newsletter, "The Weekly Weeder." John told me all that I've been missing, and will continue to miss, since membership is closed for now. The fall shares contained all manner of leafy greens, radishes, and many varieties of white and purple potatoes, sweet potatoes, winter squash, arugula and more.

The Japanese women who started it all a couple of generations ago believed it was important, too. As they said, "Put the farmer's face on the food." John and his mom have done that for me and all the lucky members of CSA's.

Leedstown, Southern Cradle of Independence

D riving up through the Northern Neck, catching glimpses of sweet and sleepy river towns, doesn't prepare you for the historic events you learn about when you happen in to a local courthouse or museum. Some of the events are widely known, but have little impact today, and some less well known, but with, I think, never-ending importance.

Leedstown is a perfect example. The ubiquitous John Smith strayed onto the shores of Leedstown in 1608 as he explored the Rappahannock River, trying to find a route to China. It was then a robust Indian village, a bit too robust. One of Smith's men died during an Indian attack. George Washington and Martha dined and slept in Leedstown a few times on their way to Williamsburg.

But far more exciting was an event of heroic proportions, and it happened a full ten years before the Declaration of Independence, when in 1765 the British Parliament imposed the notorious Stamp Act on the colonies. It was a stamp duty on all papers used for legal documents, liquor licenses, academic degrees, newspapers, pamphlets and almanacs. Well, it's been said it ignited a very early spark of revolution. Thomas Ludwell Lee, along with 115 other of Westmoreland's prominent and influential planters, furious at "taxation without representation," met at Leedstown. What resulted, after impassioned discussion and debate, is what is known today as the Leedstown Resolves, signed February 27, 1766, petitioning King George to do away with the Stamp Act. The original Leedstown Resolves manuscript is believed to be in Richard Henry Lee's handwriting and is preserved by the Virginia Historical Society. Among those 115 who signed Lee's document were six Lees, five Washingtons, and Spence Monroe, father of President James Monroe.

While all six of the resolutions making up the Leedstown Resolves have the glorious ring of freedom, this, the third, is my favorite:

> As the Stamp Act does absolutely direct the property of the people to be taken from them without their consent expressed by their representatives and as in many cases it deprives the British American subject of his right to trial by jury; we do determine, at every hazard, and paying no regard to danger or to death, we will exert every faculty, to prevent the execution of the said Stamp Act in any instance whatsoever within this colony. And every abandoned wretch, who shall be so lost to virtue and public good, as wickedly to contribute to the introduction or fixture of the Stamp Act in this colony, by using stamped paper, or by any other means, we will, with the utmost expedition, convince all such profligates that immediate danger and disgrace shall attend their prostitute purposes.

So, is it any wonder that Leedstown, right here in the Northern Neck, is called the "Southern Cradle of American Independence?"

Heathsville's Tavern

In the seventeenth and early eighteenth centuries, colonial taverns were not just the place for food and lodging and entertainments, they were the places for business transactions, and the latest news. Court proceedings and monthly court days were just about the biggest events in early American villages and towns; the Northern Neck was no exception.

Located in Heathsville in Northumberland County is Rice's Hotel/Hughlett's Tavern, which has been called the quintessential colonial Virginia courthouse tavern, an "architectural jewel." The two-story wood frame building, sitting among mulberry trees and close to the local circuit court, opened its doors to its very first customer in the 1790s and served as a tavern and hotel for the court and townspeople.

According to historian Robert E. Robinson, like other courthouse taverns in Virginia during the colonial era and later, patrons came because of the proximity to the courthouse. When the court sat at Northumberland's courthouse, across the road from the tavern, judges, lawyers and their clients, court clerks, sequestered jurors, and yes, members of the press, found food, drink, and shelter there.

When it expanded into a hotel in the 1830s, they continued to come, along with traveling salesmen, teamsters, steamboat passengers, and truck drivers. As a rule, local people did not go to the hotel.

This oldest surviving courthouse tavern in Virginia has been designated a historic landmark. How it has survived is the story of a dedicated group of volunteers known as The Tavern Rangers. The Tavern Rangers grew from the first volunteers in 1992, who cleared the weeds and overgrowth covering the hotel and tavern, to today's hundreds of Tavern Ranger volunteers, doing everything to restore and maintain the building and grounds of the place—basically, the cleaning, clearing, rebuilding. They even recovered old bricks in and around Heathsville to build the walkways.

Seeing it today, in its restored glory, it's hard to believe it was ever tumbledown. The Rangers also built an authentic colonial blacksmith shop for honest-to-goodness blacksmithing and the teaching of blacksmithing. There's a restaurant in the tavern proper, and, according to the foundation, a restaurant open to the public is a major factor in bringing the tavern back to life as the center of the community. A gift shop, The Tavern Store, was established in 1995 to raise funds for maintaining this unique place. All of this has taken more than fifteen years to accomplish. Hughlett's Tavern/Rice's Hotel, still a place to meet and eat, since the 1790s, right here, on the Northern Neck.

Westmoreland, from Champagne to the Berries

When I think of what might represent, to me, the very height of luxury in the world of comestibles, I guess I would say champagne and strawberries. If I were asked what my favorite form of entertainment is, an easy answer for me is theater; the ambiance I favor—as close to water as I can get; one of my special areas of interest—history. You can find them all in their natural state in just one of the four counties of the Neck—Westmoreland.

Some of these Westmoreland gems you may have heard of. Some are those "best kept secret" types known to a few who don't want to share them for fear of overexposure. The county's 252 square miles is packed with happenings, from the past and reaching into the future.

First, the "champagne" (known also, of course, as "sparkling wine" everywhere but the Champagne provinces of France). A superb sparkling wine is available for your tasting at the award-winning Ingleside Winery in Oak Grove, which is not really a village, but a crossroads.

The berries, of course, are hand picked at Westmoreland Berry Farm, where you do the pickin' while the kids pet the animals.

Nature has been generous to this county, as it has to all of the Neck. Right next door to the berry farm is the Voorhees Nature

Preserve. It has trails with lovely views of the Rappahannock River. And it's a bird watcher's paradise, home to bald eagles and many species of other birds. Westmoreland State Park sits along the Potomac River, near the former homes of both George Washington and Robert E. Lee. And folks come just for the fabulous view of the river from Horsehead Cliffs.

Kinsale is too tiny to have the designation of town, but it is the oldest seaport on the Virginia side of the Potomac River. Its museum traces Kinsale's history and is the starting point for a charming walking tour of this old village.

Community theatre is another surprise, and it just doesn't get any better. The Westmoreland Players were organized about twenty-eight years ago, headed up by Glen and Joy Evans. The group recently won the Best Community Theatre in Virginia award. Notable too are the Westmoreland storytellers, an African-American group who remind us of the history of their people.

It's Westmoreland's history that truly impresses. It was established in 1653 and is home to George Washington's birthplace; Stratford Hall plantation, home of Robert E. Lee, and all those other famous Lee boys; our fifth President James Monroe was born in Westmoreland; the family of Alexander Graham Bell had a summer home in Colonial Beach, the Bell House, which still stands today. Sloan Wilson, author of The Man in the Gray Flannel Suit, retired and died in Colonial Beach. And John Dos Passos wrote his trilogy U.S.A. while summering there.

The history doesn't stop. Someone, somewhere, is busy making history that we'll learn about one day, that took place right here on the Northern Neck.

Caledon, Birthplace of Eagles

Back in 1936, Virginia became the first state to open an entire park system on the same day. Today, Virginia has forty-nine state parks, and they are all truly Virginia's treasures. Four of those state parks are in the Northern Neck: Lake Anna, Westmoreland, Belle Isle, and Caledon, Caledon being my personal all-time favorite. It's actually a designated national natural landmark in King George County and it's home to the largest concentration of bald eagles on the East Coast. The area has an almost surreal feel to it, with its bluffs overlooking the Potomac River.

Caledon is spread out on more than 2,500 acres of undeveloped forestland, and the managers of the park have divided it into zones, aimed at accomplishing their sole mission: to protect the American bald eagle. In one zone there are classes and, of course, exhibits relating to the bald eagles, as well as to the plant life in this enormous undeveloped forest. Also in this zone, hiking and field trips begin.

Then there are the two zones specifically dedicated to the eagles: the eagle wildlife area and the eagle impact zone along the shoreline of the Potomac River and in the marsh and wetlands. That's where the eagles are most highly concentrated during the summer roosting and winter nesting periods. To keep the eagles from being disturbed during these critical times, no visitors are permitted. Another critical time is from

April through October and there is a "no boating zone, except for commercial fishing boats, that extends 1,000 feet into the Potomac so that the baby eagles as well as the mature birds can do their foraging and roosting."

The five hiking trails are open year round, except the Boyd's Hole Trail, which is closed in summer so that the young birds can perfect their hunting and fishing skills. But there are a limited number of tours of these eagle areas offered by Caledon mid-June through August. Beginning in October through March 31, Boyd's Hole Trail is open, taking hikers through the sensitive eagle habitat, and spotting the eagles soaring is an awesome sight.

The Founding Fathers chose the bald eagle as the national symbol on June 20, 1782, for its long life, great strength and majestic looks. It seems to me, there's something uncommonly interesting that here, in the Northern Neck, birthplace of presidents, you also have this place called Caledon, where our national symbol has found a safe place for its birthplace and its future.

Yeocomico Church, Through the Wicket Door

It's been called one of the most wonderful—and overlooked—of America's colonial buildings. It's a tiny church, on a very small road in Westmoreland County overlooking the Yeocomico River near Kinsale and Hague, Virginia. The Yeocomico Episcopal Church, built in 1706 and today a national historic landmark, celebrated its three hundredth anniversary in 2006.

If you are a church crawler, finding and exploring ancient churches, you will discover that this one is a gem. It was described by Bishop William Meade in *Old Churches and Families Of Virginia* this way: "The architecture is rough but very strong, its figure that of a cross, in the midst of some aged trees and surrounded by a brick wall; it cannot fail to be an object of interest to one who has a soul with sympathy for such scenes." The church's claim to its not-so-modest fame is based not just on its architectural features, like its rare and fabulous entrance door, but for the procession of parishioners who have passed through it.

First, the door. It is massive, probably a thousand pounds, and so wide three folks abreast can pass through. It's a rare wicket door, a smaller door within a much larger door, the smaller used in bad weather to keep the cold air out. It's the only wicket door known in colonial America.

But it is the people who passed through the door that truly interest me, and as I read more about the church, I found myself making up a rhyme: "Through the wicket door, came the wicked and the pure." Was I right?

Well, I soon learned that the parishioners ranged from prostitutes to patriots and lots in between. First, the former, whose bad deeds ended up being good for the church, economically speaking. It happened in 1706 when four women, Mary Franklin, Sara Hutchins, Sara Rogers and Susanne Palmer, were convicted of prostitution. Their fine was a rather unusual contribution to the new church's building fund. They each had to pay to the fledgling parish church five hundred pounds of tobacco. (I have been unable to locate any information as to how they obtained the tobacco.)

There were a few other known miscreants to have come through the church doors as well. During the War of 1812, a detachment of men who were supposed to be watching out for British forces coming down the river wandered into the church, perhaps to buoy up their spirits, though it was reported that the men used the baptismal font "as a vessel in which to prepare the excitements of ungodly mirth." It is also said that the font was rescued by "a venerable man of the Presbyterian connection." During that same war, the communion table was dragged outside and used as a butchering block, but happily it has been restored since then and is safely back in the church.

As might be expected, the now famous folk far outnumbered the infamous that passed through the doors of the Yeocomico church. Mary Ball Washington used to ride to church, not by carriage, but horseback, and son George Washington was baptized at this church, most likely from the very same font used almost a century later by those merrymakers. Robert Carter, grandson of Robert "King" Carter, was an early parishioner, along with the Lees and so many of early America's patriots. Today, the church, lovingly restored, continues to be a welcoming house of worship, and it's here, on the Northern Neck.

Strat-by-the-Ford

My favorite old family of the Northern Neck and Virginia history are the Lees, and Richard Henry and Francis Lightfoot Lee are my favorite offspring of that prolific family. (They were the only two brothers to have signed the Declaration of Independence, but it was their personalities that have put them in my "favorites" column.)

The story of their birthplace, Stratford Hall Plantation in Westmoreland County, reflects for me the acquisitiveness and perhaps even a sense of entitlement that runs through the stories of the men who became great landowners.

There were lots of Lees born at Stratford, all with terrific stories to tell, but it was Thomas Lee who might be credited with starting it all, at least on the banks of the Potomac.

He was a founder of the Ohio Company, and an acting governor of Virginia. Like most prominent men of the 18th century, he was a land lover, land speculator, and providentially for him, a land agent. For a while he had his eyes on property owned by the Pope family, particularly the land overlooking the Potomac, with its great bluffs offering spectacular views of the river. It is said that he let it be known that "he wanted those clifts [sic]," and evidently, what Thomas wanted, Thomas got. And he got it rather dramatically.

According to Miriam Haynie's *The Stronghold*, one day in 1716, someone representing the Pope family called on Thomas

Lee and handed him, not a calling card, but a handful of earth and a twig. With these ancient symbols of land, 1450 acres was transferred from the Popes to Thomas Lee. Of course, later on, there were papers to be signed and some payment made. A year later, he bought more land for what he called and we now call Stratford Hall Plantation. Why Stratford? Probably because his grandfather, Richard Lee the immigrant, once owned an estate in England called Strat-by-the-Ford.

Lee borrowed more than just the name from his forbears: he built his new home much like the manor houses of England, this one like an "H" shaped fortress, with two-inch thick walls, strong enough to hold enemies at bay. The magnificent manor house was built with thousands and thousands of bricks, all made on the property. By some accounts, it took about five years to build and by the time he was done, about 1738, there on the bluffs of the Potomac River was, in addition to the magnificent manor house, a wharf, grist mill, stables, and quarters for the slaves and indentured servants. There were other English-inspired additions, like the *ha ha wall*. No, I didn't know what that was, so of course, I "Googled" it, and came up with "the quirky breed of walls built in the 17th and 18th Century on country estates of the landed gentry…, constructed so as to be invisible from the house, ensuring a clear view across the estate with their walls of sunken stone." In Lee's case, it ensured a clear view of the cliffs he loved.

Today, you can get a clear view of the entire estate. It's all still there, a National Historic Landmark managed as a working farm by the Robert E. Lee Memorial Association. After costumed interpreters lead you through the house, you can stroll through the lovingly restored gardens, walk the trails to the bluffs of the Potomac River, and even watch the miller at work at the restored gristmill. If the season is right, you can have lunch or dinner in the charming log cabin dining room of the Stratford Hall Plantation, one of those "must sees," right here on the Northern Neck.

The Robert O. Norris Bridge

The year 1957 marked the completion of dozens of architectural and engineering feats: like the Lincoln tunnel, connecting Manhattan to New Jersey; like the Cologne opera house, connecting music lovers to great music; like the Hampton Roads Bridge-Tunnel connecting the city of Norfolk to the city of Hampton; and like the Robert O. Norris Bridge, crossing the Rappahannock River and connecting Lancaster County in the Northern Neck to Middlesex County and beyond.

The other architectural feats may be more dramatic, but I think none of these "connectors" has been more life changing than the Norris Bridge. It came into being thanks to the efforts of then Sen. Robert O. Norris who, it is said, wouldn't pass legislation for the Hampton Roads project unless the Rappahannock River bridge was part of the mix.

August 30, 2007 marked its fiftieth anniversary, and there are many people who remember the grand opening—the grand crossing. Some remember it with romantic sadness because it was the end of the ferry trips from Grey's Point to White Stone; some remember it because it was the end of isolation and the beginning of real opportunities.

My friend Ruby Lee Norris is a living, breathing bridge, from the past to today's Neck; and yes, she is related to Robert O.—he was her father's cousin. She had lots of relatives in

Lancaster County and she lived in Middlesex. She remembers back in the thirties, when she got her first teaching position. It was in Kilmarnock and the best practical solution to the then-bridgeless commute was to board with a family in Kilmarnock, then on weekends have her landlady take her to the ferry to cross the river, where her father would meet her. She would spend the weekend at home in Topping, then return to Lancaster for the school week. Ruby Lee Norris remembers how tough it was for young people to find jobs, unless they wanted to work on the water. And it was particularly tough for women.

The bridge slowly changed all that, and it changed the demographics of the Northern Neck. As it carried young folks away, it opened up a new gateway, and easy access for visitors, frequently an older generation of visitors—retirees and wannabe retirees—who fell in love with the area, bought summer homes, then became full-time residents.

Lately, a funny thing has been happening on the way to the Neck, and many believe it's a demographic shift. As the Robert O. Norris Bridge hits its boomer years, it's carrying more and more real live boomers, not just to visit, but also to live and work here in the Northern Neck. Some have found that working from home, computer commuting, gives them the best of both worlds: a laid-back work environment, with their boat docked close by. Some are starting new businesses, helping to breathe new life into the area. The bridge is, like many boomers, in need of a bit of a lift—some say a total makeover is in order—but that doesn't diminish its role in bridging the gap, between counties, lifestyles and generations.

Kinsale

T here is a village on the southern coast of Ireland called Kinsale. It overlooks the lovely River Bandon, and its history goes back many hundreds of years.

There is a village on the Eastern coast of the Northern Neck, the oldest seaport on the Virginia side of the Potomac River. It was established back in 1706, and it too is called Kinsale. In Gaelic that means "head of salt water" and "our" Kinsale also overlooks a river—two, in fact—the Yeocomico, and the Potomac River beyond.

Needless to say, I have been looking for connections to the Kinsale of Ireland, and indeed I found one, but it isn't a happy tale. The story goes like this.

During the War of Independence, the crews of many American vessels were held prisoner in a fort in Kinsale, Ireland, where the conditions were dreadful. Help came from a Presbyterian minister and a Quaker merchant named Reuben Harvey of County Cork. They apparently had friends in high places, and through their influence, conditions improved. President George Washington heard about their good deed and in 1783, he thanked Harvey for "his exertions in relieving the distresses of such of our fellow citizens as were prisoners in Ireland."

Today, Ireland's Kinsale and the fort where prisoners were kept are tourist attractions. In the Northern Neck's Kinsale, long before it had a bona fide name, there was also a fort. It was built when, in 1667, Virginia's General Assembly ordered one to be built on the Yeocomico to defend the Potomac River. There is no trace of it today, but lots of other bits and pieces of this old town remain, and many can be found, not surprisingly, in the Kinsale Museum, which is also the starting point for a walking tour of the old village with its Victorian era homes and stunning views.

Kinsale's historians tell us that for at least a century, the town's main business was smuggling untaxed tobacco. Later on, the War of 1812 gave the port a new role, important enough to be defended by United States naval forces. Sadly, it was to little avail. The town was sacked after the British Navy attacked the three-gun sloop, *The Asp*.

Kinsale's story doesn't end there. It took on yet another life with the beginning of the Steamboat Era and Kinsale's wharf was a busy place from the 1850s to the 1930s. Tomato canning factories added to the excitement and bustle of the town, transforming it into an important market town and steamboat landing. The walking tour brings you to the "Virginia W," a restored wooden skipjack built in 1904, considered a rare example of the Virginia built Chesapeake Bay workboat.

Back in Kinsale, Ireland, there is a lovely resort area with many traces of its long history, including documents verifying that our very own William Penn was born there. Our very own Kinsale, has its own traces of its history, not quite as long as Ireland's, but a lot closer: right here on the Northern Neck.

Helloo, Dolley

She was called "presidentress" before Zachary Taylor created the term "First Lady" to describe her, and she was much more than the nineteenth century's "hostess with the mostest." She was Dolley Payne Madison, wife of one of the Northern Neck's favorite sons, James Madison. History reminds us of her courage, and happily we have her own words. The following is from a letter Dolley Madison wrote to her sister Anna in 1814, as the British forces were approaching Washington and the President's house. (The President's residence was not officially called the "White House" until, according to online encyclopedia *Wikipedia*, "President Theodore Roosevelt established the formal name by having the *de facto* name, 'White House—Washington' engraved on the stationery in 1901.)

Now, back to Dolley's letter.

> My husband left me yesterday morning to join General Winder. He inquired anxiously whether I had courage or firmness to remain in the President's house until his return on the morrow, or succeeding day, and on my assurance that I had no fear but for him, and the success of our army, he left, beseeching me to take care of myself, and of the Cabinet papers, public and private.

Take care of them she did, saving them from destruction.

There was something else she saved, besides the President's papers. She continues her letter:

> I insist on waiting until the large picture of General Washington is secured, and it requires to be unscrewed from the wall. This process was found too tedious for these perilous moments; I have ordered the frame to be broken, and the canvas taken out. It is done! and the precious portrait placed in the hands of two gentlemen of New York, for safe keeping. And now, dear sister, I must leave this house, or the retreating army will make me a prisoner in it by filling up the road I am directed to take. When I shall again write to you, or where I shall be to-morrow, I cannot tell!

There is much more to Dolley Payne Madison than her bravery, or the desserts named after her. A recent book by historian and author Catherine Allgor points out the very real impact she had on the forming of our country. The book is *A Perfect Union: Dolley Madison and the Creation of the American Nation*. Some reviewers have suggested that the book, in a not-so-subtle way, diminishes the accomplishments of husband James. I think it simply illuminates the real role of the first First Lady. Yes, she gave tea parties and grand dinners. This excerpt from another letter to sister Anna gives us an idea of those dinners and parties.

> Where will you celebrate the Fourth of July, my dear sister? We are to have grand doings here. Mr. Van Ness is to deliver an oration, Mr.

L. says, in the woods, and the ladies are to be permitted to partake of the mirth. We have lately had a great treat in the company of a charming Prussian Baron. All the ladies say they are in love with him, notwithstanding his want of personal charms. He is the most polite, modest, well-informed, and interesting traveller we have ever met, and is much pleased with America. I hope one day you will become acquainted with our charming Baron Humboldt. He sails in a few days for France with his companions, and is going to publish an account of his travels in South America, where he lived five years, proposing to return here again. He had with him a train of philosophers, who, though clever and entertaining, did not compare to the Baron.

These grand affairs with sparkling guests weren't given, it appears, to crown herself as the queen bee of Washington. According to Allgor, "She modeled a modern form of politics.... At bottom, she created opportunities for the members of both parties to see their political opponents as full human beings." And, I would add, to give her guests the opportunity to meet somewhat exotic European nobility.

The Christian Science Monitor points out that Allgor easily captures the political landscape of early America. But even more, perhaps we can learn a bit from Mrs. Madison's tactics for bringing together people with differing views. Here's Allgor's assessment: "Mrs. Madison's style, emphasizing cooperation over coercion, building bridges instead of bunkers, could have played a useful role in today's polarized political climate...."

Dolley Payne Madison, wife of the Northern Neck's James Madison—if you have no objections, we claim you as our own.

Another Lee, Another Love

Once again, I've fallen in love with an older man with the last name of Lee. I'm really not fickle; it's just that every time I read more about a Lee man, I'm overwhelmed. This Lee was a war hero, close friend of our most famous general, not much good with money (which is putting it kindly, since he landed in debtor's prison) and of course he was married, twice. His first wife was called "divine." I call her "high maintenance Matilda." She died after only eight years of marriage. He married again a couple of years later to another beauty, much younger than he, Ann Hill Carter, from the hugely wealthy Carter clan. Both marriages brought lots more Lees into the world and one of his sons became even more famous than he.

You may have guessed that the object of my affection is Henry "Light Horse Harry" Lee, and how he got *that* name is a tale unto itself. What a tragic and, I believe, honorable life. He came back from Princeton College to fight heroically under General George Washington in the Revolutionary War, and they became fast friends, so close that Harry was asked by Congress to deliver Washington's eulogy. It became renowned, describing him as "First in war, first in peace and first in the hearts of his countrymen."

General Henry "Light Horse Harry" was also a fine statesman, was elected to the new Virginia House of Delegates and later, as Governor of Virginia.

Light Horse Harry's talents didn't include financial horse sense. His land speculations were his greatest miscalculations, landing him in that debtor's prison. Amazingly, in spite of the humiliation, he "kept on keeping on," writing in his tiny prison cell the now famous *Memoirs of the War in the Southern Department of the United States.*

What is there about a flawed hero that makes him so appealing? His first wife loved him madly, and the love was returned in kind. She, the divine Matilda, was known to have lofty tastes. She had inherited Stratford, that famed birthplace of Lees, from her father Philip, and they lived an extravagant life. Ann Hill Carter, wife number two, was a different sort. She was religious, practical, physically fragile and also very much in love with Harry. When they were at their most destitute, with Harry in prison in Montross, she would ride there each day to bring him his dinner.

His adventures didn't end there. After his release, he was nearly killed in a political riot in Baltimore when he and friends, defending the right of a free press and free speech, were beaten savagely by a mob. Harry was permanently injured, and died a few years later, with many of his dreams dying with him.

Ann moved the family from Stratford, where all their children had been born, to a small house in Alexandria, Virginia where their fifth child, Robert Edward Lee, took on the role of the man of the family. Robert Edward Lee was heartbroken even as a very young boy to leave Stratford. The boy who was to become the brilliant general of the Civil War had, like his father, unfulfilled dreams, most notably the dream to somehow buy back Stratford. But how's this for sweet irony: In 1929, The Robert E. Lee Memorial Association was formed, and bought Stratford, and today manages it as a tribute to all the Lees, particularly Robert E.

A Look Into *Fithian's Journal*

Just when you think you know a thing or two about long-ago life on the Northern Neck, something pops up on the radar screen to give yet another insight into our past. For me, it was Philip Vickers Fithian and his journal.

Reading the journal, I became aware that his observations are invaluable to understanding the men and women who were this country's first elite class. How could I have been so ignorant for so long about this forever young man, forever young because he died too early. The journal he kept from 1773 to 1774 documents his life as a plantation tutor on the eighteenth century plantation and manor house of Robert Carter III, Nomini Hall in Westmoreland County. The journal includes tantalizing observations and conclusions, sometimes wrong, and insightful details of everyday life in a part of the Colony totally unfamiliar to him.

A farmer's son and Princeton student in need of money to continue his studies for the ministry, Fithian was recruited for the tutoring job in 1773 by the then President of Princeton. He accepted, reluctantly. He was very close to his family and the New Jersey land and, above all else, he was in love with his "dearest Laura," and so he stipulated that it would be for only one year. That time frame would enable him to earn some money and get back to his studies for the ministry in New Jersey, and to Laura.

The wealthy Virginia plantation owners of the time had an enormous respect for education, and while many of the gentry sent their children back to England for their education, some like Carter preferred having education come to them. According to the editor of *Fithian's Journal*, the planters were "determined they should not return to barbarism in the wilderness." Fithian's students on the Carter plantation would range in age from five to seventeen—five daughters, two sons and a nephew—and Fithian was expected to teach Latin, Greek, sums, and literature. He would be joined by the visiting dancing, music and riding teachers, all working hard to educate the children and "hold barbarism at bay."

We learn from his journal that plantation life was not all bucolic. There were parties and dances and lots of visiting back and forth between plantations. While he may not have particularly enjoyed these merriments (his religious background taught him to frown on dancing "and such"), permission to use Carter's library far outweighed any distaste he might feel for all this frivolous behavior. It might seem a small thing to be permitted to use the manor library, but this was no ordinary library. This impressive room was so filled with the great books of the time, that it was said that Thomas Jefferson coveted the collection. One can imagine Fithian's delight at being able to savor, in his spare time, of course, this feast of learning.

The journal also reflects Fithian's strict Presbyterian background in other ways. About Southern manners, he was impressed; about church manners, he was not. The men, according to Fithian, seemed to take Sundays and religion less seriously than folks back home in New Jersey. As a matter of fact, these Southern gentlemen gathered at the church, talked business together (on Sunday!), and frequently had to be called in to prayers.

He wrote about food (they ate lots of oysters) and fishing trips on Carter's schooner. Even their "habits of dress" didn't escape the young man's curious eyes and quick pen, though sometimes his pen outraced his good sense and led him to a few hilarious conclusions. The following is one of my favorite entries: "It is a custom among the Westmoreland ladies whenever they go from home, to muffle up their heads, and necks, leaving only a narrow passage for the eyes, in cotton or silk handkerchiefs; I was in distress for them when I first came into the colony, for every woman that I saw abroad I looked upon as ill either with the mumps or toothache." That they wrapped themselves in this way to keep the dust out of hair and face while going from place to place on horseback seemed not to have occurred to our educated young man.

His notes about the latest gossip and news, of which there was plenty, gives us a unique view into the lives of the wealthy plantation owners and their families. The dinner table, where the "who's who" of Northern Neck gentry, including Richard and Frances Lightfoot Lee, might gather, was his primary source. It was "news central" and who said what to whom was recorded in his journal. And, oh, the talk: it was eclectic and educated and might flit from philosophy, science and astronomy, to marriage, widowhood, politics and war.

One can imagine the excitement of the conversation, since Fithian's year at the plantation, 1773 to 1774, was a year filled with extraordinary happenings that became centerpieces of table talk. In one entry dated June 1774 he wrote: "Virginians are warm and active in support of the colonies." Another instance was when the Virginia House of Burgesses declared that June 1 was to be a "solemn day of fasting and prayer" in silent protest to the Boston Port Act, the British proclamation that led to the Boston Tea Party. Fithian wrote in his journal that Colonel Carter instructed the household to ignore the protest. This led Fithian to wonder in his journal if perhaps "Carter was a Courtier"—that is, if Carter was unsympathetic to rebellious thinking (he was not).

Through his journal we also get a rare kind of "onsite" look at slavery on eighteenth century plantations. In a letter to his dear friend Laura, for whom he was dreadfully homesick and later married, he wrote, "The ill treatment which this unhappy part of mankind receives here would almost justify them in any desperate attempt for gaining that civility and plenty which, though denied them, is here commonly bestowed on horses." It was some solace to him to learn, during long conversations with Mrs. Carter, that she too was unhappy with slavery.

Reading the journal is like spending the day with the family from "got up early" to "went to bed about eleven," and all the happenings in between. If you are at all interested in Virginia history, Philip Vickers Fithian's journal provides an intriguing look back to the long-ago Northern Neck.

Tangier Island

When Garrison Keillor brings us news from the mythical Lake Wobegon, he reminds us that it's "the town that time forgot, where the women are strong, the men are good looking and the children are above average." Well, there's a very real island across the Bay from the Northern Neck, a place that time forgot—and the residents like it that way. About the "above average" part, think sunsets, crabs, oysters, tranquility, and hospitality, and the number of people named Crockett, Pruitt and Parks.

The island is Tangier, the one Captain John Smith is reputed to have discovered on his forays around the Chesapeake Bay in 1608. He is supposed to have dubbed it "Tangier," some say, in honor of his time spent in Morocco. More rigorous historians have other theories.

How come so many Crocketts? Well, legend has it that in 1666, a Mr. West came along, offered its original inhabitants, the Pocomoke Indians, two overcoats in exchange for the island, and it was a deal. It wasn't noted whether they shook hands. Twenty years later, West is said to have sold part of the Island to John Crockett and his sons, and the rest, as they say, is history—or is it? There are enough conflicting stories about the beginnings and naming of Tangier and who bought it from whom that you can just choose the one that suits your fancy.

History doesn't equivocate about Tangier Island and the

very real role it played in a very real conflict, the War of 1812. Some 1,200 British soldiers occupied the island, and used it as the base for their attack on Baltimore. Before and after that time, agriculture was the way of life, but around 1840 a market for seafood began developing, and "Tangiermen," replete with their Elizabethan/Southern accents, soon became one of the great suppliers for the nation's appetite for crabs and oysters and such.

Weather and sickness have always been major problems, and the people have fought many nasty epidemics. A modern day hero began playing an enormous role in their physical health when Dr. David Nichols of White Stone began tending to their health needs, which have been great. For more than thirty years, he and his team have been going to the island by boat and small plane, today by helicopter, though still using makeshift and somewhat primitive health care facilities. That may soon change. A foundation has been created to raise money for a modern clinic on the island, in honor of Dr. Nichols, and sparked by his recent award as Country Doctor of the Year.

A visit to Tangier is an instant tonic for stressful times. No autos are on the island, and a few golf carts are a recent addition. Instead, there are "eco" tours, sunset tours, bird watching, fishing, bicycling, and you can even make arrangements to go out on the workboats, crabbing or oystering with the watermen. A good way to start is in Reedville, at the tip of the Northern Neck, where you can board the *Chesapeake Breeze* at Buzzard's Point. After about an hour of lovely cruising, you arrive at Tangier. Nearby you will probably want to have a spectacular seafood lunch at one of the few island restaurants, maybe stay over in a B & B, but most of all you will have the pleasure of experiencing the real town that time forgot, just about fourteen miles and a few centuries away from the Northern Neck.

War on the Rappahannock

The details of the War of 1812—some called it Madison's War—aren't remembered by most of us, except perhaps the war's last year or so, with the dramatic burning and sacking of Washington by British troops, and how "The Star-Spangled Banner" came to be written as Francis Scott Key watched Fort McHenry burn, and survive.

But, just to fill in memory blanks, there was more. America declared war on the British because the Madison administration and those men around him who called themselves "war hawks" had become, historians say, irritated because the British wouldn't withdraw from American territory along the Great Lakes, nor did they care much for Britain's backing of the Indians on America's frontiers. There were other irritants as well, all of them seemingly too far away to have any effect on the Northern Neck.

Not so. Historians say that in retribution for the American attack at York, Ontario, British ships, under Admiral George Cockburn, came into the Chesapeake Bay and began harassing the people living on the shores of the Bay, rivers and even creeks. Stories abound that while all the able-bodied men were fighting with the militia or the navy, the folks left behind, women and children and the elderly, bore the brunt of the attacks. Houses along the shore were plundered and livestock slaughtered. A battle was fought near the town of Kinsale on the Yeocomico

River, a tributary of the Potomac, and the *USS Asp*, sent to guard the area, was overpowered. The British then occupied and later burned down the town. Northern Neck historians tell us that many other towns were ravaged as well. Historian and author Miriam Haynie writes in her book, *The Stronghold*,

> Naval battles were taking place in the rivers. The *USS Dolphin* was captured in the Rappahannock River by the British ship *St. Domingo....* Troops were stationed at Windmill Point at the mouth of the Rappahannock where in 1814 the British made a landing and pillaged a vessel.... They were driven off by militia stationed across the creek. It was perhaps on this same trip that the raiders visited Corrotomon.... British troops went ashore and made themselves at home in the old house built by John Carter, while the officers took over the house built by his son Robert King Carter. Legend has it that the well stocked wine cellar and an abundance of fine Rappahannock oysters furnished the ingredients of an all night party.

Well, the Treaty of Ghent ended the war of 1812, but, like so many wars and their so-called endings, it seemed not to have immediately resolved any of the issues that started it. Francis Scott Key's poem, our nation's anthem, may have been the best thing that came of that war:

> Now it catches the gleam of the morning's first beam,
> In full glory reflected, now shines on the stream:
> 'Tis the star spangled banner, O! long may

it wave
O'er the land of the free and the home of
the brave!

Governor Linwood Holton,
Memory and Memoir

There's something remarkable about walking through a stand of cedar trees, knowing that hundreds of years ago, men and women on horseback, or in carriages, passed through this very area, lived and toiled here, became famous for their wealth or their political power, or were just ordinary citizens beginning to dream some of the very first of the great American dreams.

Here on the Northern Neck, we are always bumping into history, and sometimes we even have the good fortune to bump into a very alive someone who has made history, like former Governor Linwood Holton, governor of Virginia from 1970 to 1974. He now lives a creek or two away with his wife, Jinks. He came to all the local rallies when his son-in-law, Virginia's governor, Tim Kaine, was running for office, and sometimes we meet him at non-political events. He has written a memoir, *Opportunity Time*. It's a good book about a very decent man's life. The title comes, he tells us, from his morning wake-up call to his children when they were little: "Opportunity time!"

As the first Republican governor in a very long time, Linwood Holton believes that he probably did more for race relations than most others in Virginia, and it's clear that he sees that as one of his great legacies. In the chapter "Leading by Example," he tells us how he delivered what he calls the "final fatal" blow to what was known as the Byrd Machine, a network of conservative Democrats who had flouted for more than a decade the Brown vs. Board of Education decision through their policy of "massive resistance."

And this is how he did it. He writes, "On the first day of school in August 1970, our thirteen-year-old daughter Tayloe and I, at Kennedy H.S., and Jinks with Ann and Woody, age twelve and ten, at Mosby Middle school, voluntarily carried out the orders of the U. S. District Court that had been affirmed earlier that month on appeal to the U. S. Supreme Court. The orders required cross-town bussing to eliminate the effects of racial discrimination prohibited by the U. S. Constitution.... I was exuberant that morning.... Supported by a believing family, and confident that most Virginians and certainly posterity would agree, I proclaimed by one simple act that 'Virginia is part of this republic, and Virginia will comply with its laws.... In other words," he wrote, "we were putting our actions and our children where my mouth was."

The next day, a picture of Tayloe and the governor approaching the high school made the front page of *The New York Times*. Governor Holton writes, "That photograph became an icon of my administration." In his inaugural address he proclaimed, "Let our goal in Virginia be an aristocracy of ability, regardless of race, color or creed." He recounts with the greatest of pride an incident that took place in the early 1980s when he and Mrs. Holton were at the Urbanna Oyster Festival. He writes, "An old black man, rather stooped, got my attention and signaled that he had something he wanted to say to me.... I bent down to hear his words, spoken barely above a whisper: 'first Governor of all the people.'

Governor Linwood Holton, we're proud to call you neighbor, here on the Northern Neck.

The Glass House

It's been called a puzzle within a puzzle; some call it a unique encyclopedia, and if you like historic homes, this is truly unique. You won't have to worry about thick velvet ropes keeping you out of ancient rooms, replete with their elegant paintings hanging on the walls because, well, there are no paintings, or rooms, or even very many walls, at least not in the   conventional sense. But it's one of the most fascinating historic home sites for students of architecture, mystery lovers and puzzle solvers. It's Menokin, near the town of Warsaw, in the Northern Neck. It was built in 1769 for Francis Lightfoot Lee, and his bride Rebecca Tayloe. It was a lovely home and we know that because, amazingly, the original drawings for it were found in 1964   at Rebecca Tayloe's family home, Mount Airy, which was the prototype for Menokin. The Lees lived and loved there, until their deaths, ten days apart, in 1797.

Afterwards, the house had several owners, but it was falling apart, and then slowly collapsed. The folks who owned it at the time had the foresight to have all of the interior paneling, and woodwork and such removed and securely stored. Actually eighty percent of Menokin exists, in pieces. Sarah Pope, Executive Director of the Menokin Foundation calls it a giant jigsaw puzzle. The Foundation was created in 1995 to take over the management of the property, which includes hundreds of acres of forests and fields and stunning shoreline. Founding trustee W. Tayloe Murphy has been its guiding hand. Tayloe Murphy told me...."Because of my lifelong association with my cousins who have lived at Mount Airy I have become especially attached to my Tayloe ties. ...."And he might have added that his lifelong advocacy for the area has been reflected in his tenure as a member of the Virginia House of delegates from 1982 to 1999, serving on conservation related committees, and then chosen by Governor Mark Warner to serve as his Secretary of Natural Resources.

But what about the house? Now it's time for you to use your imagination. A renowned interdisciplinary team of structural architects has come up with ideas that are in line with the Foundation's vision. They have determined that the missing parts of Menokin could be rebuilt using...glass. It will be used as both an innovative construction material and as a shell that would reveal the structural and decorative elements of Menokin. Girders, joists, posts, and paneling, will be returned to their original location. Just imagine being able to see the bones of the building. What a boon to students of Colonial architecture and history. When you ask the Foundation folk, why go to all that trouble to save Menokin they say "Menokin is a nationally significant patriotic site. Until it was acquitted by the Foundation it was the only home of a Virginia signer of the Declaration of Independence that was not secured. Only Menokin, of the surviving homes of the signers, remained at risk.". Now at risk no more, this historic site with so much to offer will bring together the study of our man made and natural environment into one very remarkable place ... a 21st century glass house enabling us to peer back into the 18th century.

A "Plate" of Our Own

Charles "Chip" Jones is a very nice young man, a young man you would be proud to call your own. His roots run deep into the Northern Neck soil. His family has farmed here for a couple of generations. His love for the land and his appreciation of a way of life deepened after his first tour of duty in Iraq with the Virginia National Guard. His concern for the area deepened as well—it was getting mighty built up. How to preserve what he loved became a kind of mission.

He learned about the new Northern Neck Farm Museum, dedicated to preserving the area's agricultural heritage, and he quickly became a devoted volunteer. Another thing Chip did on his return from Iraq was to take up again a favorite pastime, driving along the byways of the area. He started noticing license plates, especially those so-called "common interest" plates. Virginia has about 200 of these and they range from plates with logos of universities to military logos, along with logos of cities and areas. He saw some from the Eastern Shore, some from Virginia Beach, but none from the Northern Neck. Chip thought there ought to be one, and thereby hangs this tale of a "win-win-win idea."

One of his friends happened to be Rob Whitman, then in the Virginia Assembly. Whitman thought a license plate for the Northern Neck was a great idea and he introduced a bill calling for it. Then he was called to serve the area in the United

States Congress, but he didn't abandon the idea of the plate. He asked Northern Neck-born state senator Richard Stuart to sponsor the bill calling for a Northern Neck license plate. He agreed, and the bill is in the House Transportation Committee waiting for approval.

Now, here's the Catch 22 we've been expecting: in order for that to happen, the DMV must receive at least 350 applications requesting a Northern Neck plate. After approval comes production, and then—this is the "win-win-win" part—after one thousand plates are sold, the DMV will allocate fifteen dollars of the annual license plate fee to an organization named in the sponsor's bill. In this case, Chip came up with yet another great idea. The recipient would be the Northern Neck Land Conservancy, whose mission embodies Chip's feelings about the area, preserving the rural character of the Northern Neck.

If you are interested in applying for this historic license plate, you can go to www.nnplate.com for an application and be part of a "win-win-win" deal: a Northern Neck license plate, a contribution to the Northern Neck Land Conservancy, and a dream come true for Chip Jones.

Chip told me that his military experience in Iraq gave him a much deeper appreciation for all those Northern Neck folks, famous and not-so, whose dreams helped shape this country.

We think there will be a lot of folks working to make Chip's dream a reality. It's not a big dream really, but it's his dream, and if we make it our dream too, well, it's a small thank you to Chip, who expects to be redeployed to Iraq. Our prayers are with you, Chip. Come home safely to your much-loved Northern Neck, where so many American dreams have come true.

About the Author

Thea Marshall is a professional writer, broadcaster, actor, and producer, with life long experience in all forms of communication from print to theater to radio and television. She is well known in Virginia's Northern Neck as a broadcaster and as regular columnist and contributor to various magazines.

Ms. Marshall writes and broadcasts original commentaries on and about the people, places, history, culture and current issues relating to the Northern Neck for National Public Radio's Richmond/Northern Neck stations, WCVE/WCNV.

Before her work at NPR, Marshall was the host of the award winning, hour long "Thea Marshall Show" featuring interviews and her commentaries about the region.

While based in Washington, D.C., she formed Thea Marshall Communications Inc., writing, voicing and producing dozens of public affairs radio, television and cable productions for a variety of clients, including AARP, The Communications Workers of America, The National Pasta Association, Riggs National Bank, NEA, and many more. The programs were aired on National Public Radio, Cable, commercial broadcast stations and PBS. Her programs on nursing home abuse won major awards, and letters of commendation to her from senators on the Senate Aging Committee were read into the Congressional Record. Her programs on women and farming in Africa won national attention and major national awards.

She has written a series of one woman shows, including "Scandalous Dorothy Parker," "Speaking of Love," "The Magnificent Rebel, Edna St. Vincent Millay" and "The Many Faces of Woman." She has performed them locally and nationally.

Ms. Marshall has lived in Virginia's Northern Neck since 1989.